They Call Me "THE BIG E"

Elvin Hayes and Bill Gilbert

Prentice-Hall, Inc.
Englewood Cliffs, N.J.

They Call Me "The Big E"
by Elvin Hayes and Bill Gilbert

Copyright © 1978 by Elvin Hayes and Bill Gilbert

Printed in the United States of America

Prentice-Hall International, Inc., London
Prentice-Hall of Australia, Pty. Ltd. Sydney
Prentice-Hall of Canada, Ltd., Toronto
Prentice-Hall of India Private Ltd., New Delhi
Prentice-Hall of Japan, Inc., Tokyo
Prentice-Hall of Southeast Asia Pte. Ltd., Singapore
Whitehall Books Limited, Wellington, New Zealand

10 9 8 7 6 5 4 3 2 1

Library of Congress Cataloging in Publication Data

Hayes, Elvin,
    They call me "The Big E."

    1. Hayes, Elvin   2. Basketball players
—United States—Biography.   3. Religion and sports.
I. Gilbert, Bill,   joint author.   II. Title.
GV884.H32A34   796.32'3'0924 [B]   77-26321
ISBN 0-13-917054-5

To my mother and father and the Hayes family,
To Erna and her family,
To John Calvin,
To Guy Lewis and Harvey Pate,
To Al Ross, my lawyer,
To the Baughers of Maryland,
To the Fine family of Milwaukee, Wisconsin, and
To all of my other dear friends
This book is sincerely dedicated.
And I give all the glory and honor to God.

Contents

Introduction

It isn't easy writing a book with a professional basketball player. His schedule is your enemy. Writing a book with a pro football player, as I did with Mike Curtis of the Washington Redskins when he was leading the Baltimore Colts' defense, was easier. Play Sunday, home all week. His house Tuesday, your house Thursday. Easy.

viii

But when your subject is an NBA star, life is more complicated. Here today, gone tomorrow. And when he is here, he's playing a game.

So you get together as best you can, looking for windows in the schedule where you can climb through with your tape recorder and steal an hour or two of your man's time from the insane NBA schedule.

With Elvin Hayes it gets even worse. He is probably the most sought athlete in Washington—and the most committed to his community. His rare chances for a night at home during the October-to-May marathon usually are wiped out with a speech to a community group. He gives far more of his time to his neighbors than any other member of the Washington Bullets, and asks their Director of Press Relations, Marc Splaver, for more. He almost never gets paid but he keeps on doing it, and he's a sucker for kids' groups. If the kids want him, he'll be there.

So writing a book with a superstar, with that kind of schedule and popularity, becomes a test of your ingenuity in getting enough time to develop material for a book of 75,000 words.

Elvin Hayes couldn't make every date I suggested. And sometimes when he thought he could, he had to cancel at the last minute. But he made every one possible and always made up any postponements, sometimes even squeezing in a session at his house between practice at two in the afternoon and packing to catch a six o'clock plane.

He was at my house one beautiful Sunday afternoon in May. The Bullets had been eliminated from the playoffs by the Houston Rockets in the second round. He was "on vacation" and not liking it a bit. And the press was ripping him apart in an episode that the reader will learn about later in these pages, following which one of the reporters involved was transferred to other assignments.

My wife, Lillian, and our 13-year-old son, David, were expressing their support for him. The NBA star, knowing the boy's hopes for a career as an athlete, looked at David, flashed a wide smile, and said, "That's the price you pay. You'll find out if you get there."

That's one of the things you notice about Elvin Hayes. He accepts many things better than a lot of us. This same guy who says he starts every game promising himself to destroy his opponent can also accept the outcome, whatever it is. He may not like it. He may be determined to change the result the next time out. But for the time being, he accepts it.

Through it all he remains as unpretentious as ever, showing up at your house in a Bullets T-shirt, jeans and sneakers, stretching his long legs across the den floor and talking with as much enthusiasm about your neighbor's weeping willow tree or his ranch back home near Houston as he shows in discussing basketball and religion.

Elvin Hayes is simple yet complicated, calm yet controversial, humble yet proud, sensitive yet thick-hided, meek before his God but a fighter under the backboard.

He prefers to be your friend because of what he is as a person, not because he's a sports celebrity. His family. Those who like him for what he is as a person. His career now. His life after basketball. His religion. His God. These mean the most to Elvin Hayes.

If you're an author writing a book with him, these are the things you notice and remember about him. After more than six months of so many visits and all those telephone conversations, you know that the tall man is also a deep man.

Bill Gilbert
Washington, D.C.

POVERTY AND PREJUDICE, VIOLENCE AND TOM SAWYER

When Willis Reed, now the coach of the New York
Knicks, was their star center, he used to stretch things slightly
if people asked how tall he was. "I'm somewhere
between 6-9 and 6-10," he'd say, "but I'm closer to 6-10
than I am to 6-9. I was always taught that when
something is more than half, you go to the next whole
number. So I consider myself 6-10."

When you ask Elvin Hayes the same question, he
tells you, "Six-nine and a half."

As you get to know Hayes, the superstar
forward of the Washington Bullets, you realize such answers
tell you something about the man they call The Big E.
He is direct and honest, and he lays it right out there for
you. "Six-nine and a half." Not "6-10." Not even
"almost 6-10." "Six-nine and half." That's Elvin Hayes,
who tells you a great deal about himself in his candid
and controversial answers to your questions, and in other
ways as well.

As you're writing a book with him, a scene
comes back to you. You're having lunch with Elvin, just the
two of you, at a motel near Fort Meade, Maryland (the
Bullets' training camp), just outside Washington. At the next
table is Hayes' boss, Coach Dick Motta, talking to the
General Manager of Radio Station WTOP, which broadcasts
the Bullets' games. Kevin Grevey and Mitch Kupchak
are at the table on the other side, two young and rising stars
hoping to make it as big in the National Basketball
Association as Elvin Hayes has.

The two of you finish the meal. Just before you
leave, Elvin Hayes gets up, his long, trim frame unwinding
out of the chair as he reaches for the pitcher of iced tea.
Hayes picks up the pitcher and carries it to the next table.
There the superstar, voted College Player of the Year as
a senior and a member of the NBA All-Star team all nine
years he's been a pro, refills the iced-tea glasses of
Grevey and Kupchak, the two young hopefuls.

2

Elvin Hayes is a man of refreshing contradictions. He is a highly paid athlete who thinks today's athletes make too much money. He is one of the most prominent members of a professional sport in an age when pro athletes are considered greedy and concerned only about money, yet he is a deeply religious man who carries his Bible with him on road trips and is thinking about becoming a minister when he retires from pro basketball.

He is the object of constant publicity, yet he prefers the privacy of his home, his wife Erna and his three children, Elvin Jr., Erna Elisse, and Erica—the kids clinging to his arms and legs, with the visitor wondering who's enjoying it more, the kids or Daddy.

Family

He is a quiet man who does not enjoy controversy, yet he always has the courage, the compulsion, to speak out on issues—as he does in these pages—and controversy has been his frequent although unsought companion.

Elvin Hayes grew up a black man in the white man's world of northern Louisiana—his neighborhood was called "Niggertown" by blacks as well as whites—where the rain turned the dirt street into a muddy stream and you could bet that somebody would get killed every Saturday night in a fight. Yet he deplores violence of any kind and hates no man of any color.

Elvin Hayes now moves in the comfortable world of the star professional athlete, traveling across the country and even overseas in the fastest jets, staying at the finest hotels, using the best athletic equipment money can buy. Yet to play the first basketball game of his life, he had to slip out the back door of Eula D. Britton High School in Rayville, Louisiana, and scrounge through the trash can hoping to find an old pair of sneakers thrown away by someone rich enough to afford a new pair. He found two worn-out shoes, considered himself lucky and hurried back inside to play his very first basketball game—in two sneakers from the trash. They were both for the left foot.

Poor

3

Elvin Hayes, the product of these contradictions because he has lived them, remembers all of them, yesterday's and today's, with a recall both instant and total, which tells much about the making of the man.

People have always told me I should write a book someday. I think they feel that way because they just assume that all big-name athletes write books sooner or later, although only a few of them really do. But I guess they've also made the suggestion to me over the years because my friends know I'm the kind of guy who gives a lot of thought to a lot of things and is always willing to talk about them—on the record.

I've always felt the same way, that maybe I should write a book. I do have some things to say, not just about today's issues in sports—and there are a lot of them I'd like to talk about—but to straighten out a few things that happened earlier in my career, such as my first few years in the NBA when some people tried to saddle me with a reputation as a troublemaker, and some recent attempts to do it again. I'd like to set the record straight on that and a few other things, too.

But I don't have in mind writing an angry book, because I am not an angry person. Besides clearing up the past and speaking out on some of today's problems in sports, I thought I would also enjoy talking about some other things—my boyhood in Louisiana, which was so much fun even in all the prejudice and poverty in the poor black section of a rural Southern town in the 1950's. My college days at Houston and my battle against Kareem Abdul-Jabbar in the game against UCLA in what many people consider the greatest college basketball game ever played. My religious and moral beliefs and concerns. And some stories and comments about life in the NBA.

4

Bill Russell is from my part of Louisiana, the northeast corner. Unlike me, he says he is bitter now about his memories of his hometown, Monroe, 24 miles from my home in Rayville. Even after all his years away from there, finishing his boyhood in Oakland, California, and his years in college and with the Boston Celtics and as coach of the Seattle Supersonics. Bill says he minds the prejudice of those years more now than he did at the time. "When I was young," he says, "I just assumed that was the way it had to be."

It was the same way with us over in Rayville. But I haven't grown bitter about it over the years. I know we were mistreated. I knew it at the time, too. You couldn't help being aware of it. The white folks would hire you to work all day picking cotton, then sometimes they'd fire you fifteen minutes before your eight hours were up on some phony charge so they wouldn't have to pay you. Your own community high school would win the state championship and you'd be voted the most valuable player in the tournament, and you'd never get your name in the paper—because black schools and black players were never mentioned in the paper. You'd be walking down the street and a white policeman would come around the corner and say, "Nigger, go down to jail and lock yourself up." And you'd go.

And the poverty was as bad as the prejudice. For a long time we didn't have indoor plumbing, and when we finally got it—and a telephone, too—we thought we were rich, even though the phone was on a party line. Christmas meant you got a toy—one toy, and you went to church as many times as possible on Christmas Day, to Rankin Chapter Methodist and Mount Zion and others, because they gave you a basket of fruit. And you never got a present on your birthday because your family couldn't afford one.

But I'm not bitter today about either the preju-

5

dice or the poverty. That's just the way things were. I guess I *would* be bitter if I had been denied the opportunity to work my way out of that life and up to a better life. But I wasn't denied it. I was offered all the opportunity in the world thanks to the University of Houston and my coach there, Guy Lewis, and some other great people there, and some people in the NBA and some others who had a strong and positive influence on me when I was growing up back home in Rayville. That's why I'm grateful instead of bitter, and that's why I feel America is the greatest country in the world—and I'm not afraid to say it.

It's kind of strange, really. I loved my life in Rayville, but from the time I was in the ninth grade I knew I just had to get out of there someday. I was having a great time, but somehow I knew there was a better life out there, beyond Rayville and northern Louisiana and Texas close by, and I knew that a better life somewhere was waiting for anyone who was willing to work hard to get it. I made up my mind at that early age to reach up to that better life, black or not, poor or not. I'd walk from Niggertown to U.S. Route 80 and watch the cars with out-of-state tags go by, right past Rayville, or I'd go to a gas station and talk to the people just passing through or I'd read about faraway places in magazines, and I'd swear to myself that someday, somehow, I was going to go to a better life. I had no way of knowing that basketball was going to be the vehicle. All I knew was I was going to find some kind of a vehicle.

At the time I first became convinced that someday I would have to leave my hometown, I had no way of knowing a lot of things. After all, I was only fifteen years old. The one thing I knew was that I was all of a sudden facing a very different life, even at that tender age, than what I had known up to that age. My father had just died. I was only in the ninth grade. I wished

6

then, and I still wish today, that I had known him longer. I was extra close to him for those few years God let me know him, but I often wish I had been able to have my father until he reached old age so that I could have known him more and enjoyed him longer into my own adult years, the way most people are able to enjoy their parents.

For some reason I wasn't to be that fortunate, and my father left us at that early time in his middle age. It was ironic that I was so young when he died, me the baby of the family and the one who was to know him for fewer years than any of my brothers and sisters. I say ironic because when I was born I wasn't expected to live, and it was my father who refused to accept the doctor's gloomy prediction that I was too weak and sickly to survive. It was my father who used to pour milk down me night and day. It was my father who spoiled me, knowing that the doctor said I was too small to survive. And Dad was the one who let me charge candy at the store next to our house on Texas Street and smothered me with so much special treatment that my brothers and sisters didn't like me very much my first few years. And when I started school I was too spoiled to adjust and I spent the whole first grade crying. I was like that—shy and lonely—until my junior year in high school.

That's why I took the death of my father extra hard. He meant so much to me, especially at that tender age, that his death really took something out of me for a long time. The blow was even harder because my brother-in-law had died just before my father. I used to follow that guy's footsteps and stay with him like his shadow. He died at a very early age, then Dad died right after him. After that, even though I was still only in my early teens, nothing could bother me or hurt me. Even today I don't show my emotions very much when someone dies. I don't cry at funerals. Not that I won't cry, because sometimes I will, but those two deaths, so close to each other and taking two people who meant so much to me, made me almost immune to showing any emotions about death.

I made it through those uncertain first few months and years, always small for my age but getting healthier all the time, thanks to my parents, especially my father and all that milk and food he kept pumping into me. No one had any reason to believe I would become tall, or even of average height. My father was only 5 feet 5 inches tall, and my tallest brothers and sisters are only 5-7. I stayed weak and small until the eleventh grade, but then it became apparent I was going to take after my mother's side of the family, where some of my uncles are 6-7, 6-9, 6-11.

My father was black, and so is my mother. That may sound obvious, but back in that part of Louisiana there are some fascinating mixtures. That's Creole country, where they speak English and broken French. In my mother's family, my great-grandfather was black but my great-grandmother was Indian. My mother's parents were both black, but my grandmother on my father's side was Indian and my grandfather was white. Some of my first cousins there speak nothing but Creole.

Life there was sort of a combination of Tom Sawyer and the inner-city ghetto. We did the happy-go-lucky things that kids in small towns out in the country do, but violence was always with us. People were always getting killed on Saturday nights in Niggertown. They'd slave all week on one of the big cotton farms, breaking their backs from dawn to dusk. Then they'd come into town on Saturday night with their week's pay, knowing they could get drunk and get some relief from their week's boring and exhausting work. Then, in their drunken state, they'd try to show they were tougher

8

than the next guy and somebody would wind up getting shot to death or stabbed to death.

It wasn't just the adults, either. Seven or eight of my buddies were killed in fights when we were kids. One time we were standing on the curb just talking, not doing anything wrong. In fact, not doing anything period. Then a white kid comes up and hits one of my buddies and kills him. Just like that. And we weren't able to do anything about it because the white people who ran things didn't care. Just another dead nigger.

The most violent sight I ever saw in Rayville was one morning in the summertime when I was a teenager and I went down into the middle of Niggertown to board one of the trucks to be taken out to pick cotton all day. It was four in the morning, and while I was waiting at the back door of the Busy Bee bar I heard a fuss inside. I looked through the window of the door just in time to see a man whip out a gun and shoot two men dead right in front of my eyes. Just like all the other cases, these men had been playing and drinking all night and got to arguing and one of them decided to kill somebody and that was that.

Nothing much ever happened to the people who did the killing. We were just niggers anyhow. They'd take the guy who had done the shooting to jail, and the next morning one of the white cotton farmers would show up and say, "You got one of my niggers in here?" The jailer would say yes and they'd go get him and the cotton farmer would say, "Nigger, go get on my tractor." And the poor old guy would walk outside and climb on that tractor and get carried back to his week of picking cotton with no relief—until next Saturday night.

I picked cotton, too, just like everybody else. I did everything you can do to cotton—picked it, chopped it, pulled it, baled it.

I steered clear of all that violence and bloodshed

9

myself, though. I kept hearing enough of it and seeing enough of it that I didn't want to get myself killed or ruined for life. Like the time the worst man in Rayville decided to kill some guy who had given him trouble, so he set himself up in a saloon with two shotguns and three pistols waiting for his enemy. But the police flushed him out of the saloon and ordered him to surrender. Instead the guy came out with guns blazing and was gunned down in the middle of the dusty street, just like in any Hollywood Western.

The one person all of us avoided was the law officer in Rayville, a white man. He was so rough and mean that when he turned the corner at Perkins Store and hit the street sign with his stick, any drunk black man would stiffen right up and walk down that street just as straight as you please. He didn't call you anything but nigger. If he wanted to talk to you about a shooting or anything else, he'd just say, "Nigger, go up and lock yourself up in jail." And the poor black guys would do it, even if the jail was ten blocks away. Or he'd say, "Nigger, go get in my car." And they'd go and get in and sit there like an obedient dog—in the back seat.

He died in 1964, and you couldn't convince some blacks for two or three years afterward that he was really dead.

All of this had an effect on me, and still does. When you grow up in that kind of an environment, when the fascinating thing about the weekend was wondering who would get killed and when it was routine to see some guy lying in the middle of the street in a pool of blood, you can go one of two ways. You can grow up thinking this sort of thing is natural and acceptable, so you start doing the same. And you wind up on a treadmill, never getting anywhere but drunk and broke at least, or dead. Or you grow up realizing the evil and stupidity in that kind of existence and you acquire a

10

deep respect for human life, one probably far deeper than people who have never been exposed to the weekly bloodshed and killing that you've always lived with. That's the way I went, knowing that this just is not the way God meant human beings to live.

The kids were exposed to this bad influence early. One of the first fights I ever had was when I was seven years old. It was with a girl the same age who lived in our neighborhood. We were fussing about something and she smacked me across the nose with a brick, the first time I ever broke my nose. I ran straight home and hid from my mother and repaired the damage myself and never told her until only a few years ago after several seasons in the NBA. I kept my secret from her all those years, even though my nose bled every day, especially in the summer. But human nature has a way of evening things up. Two weeks after that girl bashed in my nose with that brick, a grown man hit her over the head with a Coke bottle and knocked her cold. In Rayville nobody was safe.

Once another boy stole my bike and hit me in the head with a wooden plank. I saw four of everything that night. I waited a whole month for the chance to get even. Then one day I saw this same guy near me, beyond some bushes. I crawled through the bushes and hit him in the head with another Coke bottle and had my revenge. I was determined to get even no matter how long it took.

But now, after living all my boyhood in that atmosphere, I have no desire to extract an eye for an eye. It doesn't accomplish anything and I saw enough violence and injury and blood and death over senseless arguments or pledges of revenge to last me ten lifetimes or a hundred. Why risk injury or death to myself or someone else because we're arguing? I've had one fight in the NBA, with Tom Boerwinkle. He's pretty big and

11

so am I and we let each other have it for a few blows but, fortunately for both of us, it all ended before one of us had ruined his career.

I know some fans and writers think I'm too passive on this score, that I should get in there with fists flying and throw some bodies around and commit all sorts of violence and then I'll be a better player. I'm not going to do that, and if a few people who don't know any better think that makes me a coward, then that's the way it will have to be. I'm one of the league leaders every year in rebounds, and the most physical place in the world is under an NBA backboard. In 1977 I became only the twelfth player in the history of professional basketball to grab 10,000 rebounds in his career, a couple of months before my teammate, Wes Unseld, reached the same level. So I don't see how you can call either one of us a coward. Nobody ever accused Unseld of being one, so why me? And you can't say it would help my team any for me to get into some brawls, either. Every year I'm one of the league leaders in minutes played. That's where I can help my team, being out on the floor playing the game instead of on the bench injured after a fight or in the dressing room after getting kicked out by the officials.

I once got three shots in a row from John Drew of Atlanta, but I knew it wasn't intentional. So we talked it out during the game and everything was cool after that. That's how to handle that kind of situation. I have a lot of respect for my fellow players all around the league. This is their livelihood and mine. If you get into a fight and cripple a guy or ruin his career, all the "sorrys" in the world won't help him. Who's going to pay his bills for the rest of his life while he's in a wheelchair?

If I'm getting pushed around too much, I get the guy off me by talking to him or making him laugh or asking about his family. Sometimes if the guy makes a couple of baskets I tell him he's shooting well and he calms down. Any time I see a guy getting whipped up to the point where he might do something that he could regret the rest of his life, I start talking to him and loosening him up.

That's the way I've always played the game, and I've accomplished more in my career than a lot of the fighters who have come and gone and nobody remembers them. Just like all those dead and crippled guys who would shoot it out or come at you with a knife in Rayville on Saturday night. I'm not afraid of anybody, but that kind of thing just doesn't make sense—not in Rayville and not in the NBA.

With all that violence in Rayville, the most frightening experience while I was growing up came from, of all things, a basketball game. It was the Britton girls' team against the Tallulah girls, with the winner qualifying for a major tournament. I was in the seventh grade, and I couldn't wait to go to the Britton gym to see one of my first basketball games ever. I slipped in through the back, climbing through an opening above the door. I was dressed in dirty blue jeans, my hair was messed up, and my shirt was open down to my chest because it didn't have a neck button. I squeezed myself into a corner of the gym to watch the fun.

Before I knew it, a ball came bouncing toward me, headed out of bounds. I fielded it cleanly and threw it back to the ref, just as proud as I could be. I knew absolutely nothing about the rules. The referee runs over and takes the ball from me and asks, "Where are you from?"

I grinned all across my face and said, "I'm from Rayville! From Eula Britton!"

He says, "Technical foul on Rayville!"

I didn't realize the ball hadn't hit out-of-bounds before I grabbed it, and I wouldn't have known the

13

difference anyhow. You can almost imagine the result. Our girls' team lost by 1 point—the free throw which Tallulah made following the technical on me.

You can imagine how I felt, but my embarrassment and disappointment were the least of my troubles. Everybody in Rayville seemed to be out to get me after that loss, and they weren't fooling around. I was a haunted kid for weeks. Some people even threatened to kill me, and they weren't kidding. I spent every minute possible inside the house. I tried to slip out of school a few minutes early every day I got the chance, and I ran all the way home. One of the roughest guys in town smacked me every time he saw me for more than a year after that.

Because I didn't know the rules, I still had trouble understanding what I had done wrong, especially after thinking I had done everyone a favor. I knew all the girls on our team, and then I made it a point to learn who else was associated in any way with the team—for purposes of identification so I'd know what people to avoid. I avoided them all for weeks and spent a lot of time in my room, a bewildered boy. My bewilderment was increased when I kept remembering that the referee even knew who I was because he was from Rayville himself. Besides, he could have told just by looking at me that some scrawny kid like me couldn't be from Tallulah, where life was better and the folks looked a lot more slicked up than I did. But can you imagine being threatened with death over something like that? Now maybe you can see why I feel the way I do about violence and fighting.

One other incident left me almost as scared. My best friend, Ronnie Jenkins—he went on to Grambling when I went to the University of Houston—and I took the bus over to Tallulah one Sunday to see two girl friends. It cost us each two dollars round trip. It almost cost us our lives, too.

It was about five o'clock in the afternoon and we had told our dates goodbye and were headed back to the bus station, walking along and minding our own business. Now Tallulah was a bad town for us black folks. They used to say that if you were black and they didn't know you, those white cops would put you in jail and you might never come out. We believed it.

Ronnie and I were walking down the street and it was just our luck that here comes a white police officer who knows we're not from Tallulah and starts to give us the treatment.

"What are you niggers doing over here?"

Ronnie, who sometimes had more courage than he should have, said, "What's wrong? What are you talking about?"

I was getting scared stiff and started nudging Ronnie and telling him to come on, let's get down to that bus station and hop on the first thing that's moving.

But the cop got mad right away that some nigger kid would have the guts to ask him a question right back, so he says, "You gonna get smart, huh, nigger?"

Man, I thought for sure he was going to kill us right there on the spot or take us to that jail that all black people had heard about and do away with us there. I really did think we might get killed by that white cop, especially because Tallulah had such a bad reputation toward blacks in general and Rayville blacks in particular. One black man from Rayville was chased all the way from Tallulah back to Rayville and was shot sixty times during the chase.

I was remembering all this and sweating out Ronnie's short fuse and afraid he was going to get us both killed. Then the cop convinced me I was right by whipping out his gun and sticking it into Ronnie and

15

pushing him with it and I'm thinking to myself, "Oh, Lord, here I am about to go away to college, something I've been dreaming about almost all my life, and Ronnie's going to get us both killed and I'm never going to see Houston and I may not even see Rayville anymore, either."

Finally that cop says, "You niggers get on over to that bus over yonder and get out of town."

I was never so happy to obey a white cop in all my life. There was a black family waiting for the bus to start loading, so Ronnie and I went over to them and mingled in with them so we could be hiding—but it was pretty tough to hide me because I had grown to 6 feet 5 inches. That bus seemed to sit there for an eternity and I thought sure that cop was going to change his mind and come over and yank us off that bus after all. He didn't, though, and the wheels finally, finally started moving and for the next few minutes I was all in favor of bussing.

The Tom Sawyer life made up for all the violence and prejudice and poverty. I can't believe that I could have had as much fun anywhere else, and basketball wasn't even a part of it until my early teens. Until that time I was happy running and playing all over Rayville and enjoying the chickens and hogs and other animals we kept at our house on Texas Street, the house where I was born. During their early years of marriage my parents lived where they worked—right in the cotton compress owned by a group of white investors, where the larger bales from the cotton gins were compressed into smaller bales for shipping and then loaded onto freight trains.

My parents had a bed there in the compress, and that was their home. No such thing as a living room or a dining room or anything like that, just a bed and a place to cook food. Dad would work from seven in the morning until five in the afternoon, and Mom would take his place and run it from five until midnight. They were engineers supplying steam to the press that did the actual compressing. It may not have been the greatest job in the world, but when the husband has only a first-grade education and the wife only a second-grade one and you live in rural Louisiana and it's the 1940's and you're black, you take a job like that and thank the good Lord for it. Chris, Robert and Dennis were all born in the compress. After we moved to Texas Street, Arthur, Bunny and I came along, plus another sister who died in infancy.

Basketball was to be my savior as well as my ticket out of Rayville, but it was a long time in showing up. In the meantime, I played baseball more than any other sport—it was always my favorite—but we did a lot of other fun things, too, that can be experienced only by kids in a small country town. In the summers we used to get up at six o'clock and catch crickets all day long right up to seven at night. Then we'd sell them for bait, two for a penny or, if we were really ambitious, a penny each. We used to get hungry doing that all day long, so we'd sneak into a watermelon patch and steal some melons and bust them open and feast on that. We had an old swimming hole and we used to steal peaches from a white man's orchard near there until one day he caught us and started shooting at us. One guy had to have his mother pick the buckshot out of his rear end.

We had a big fig tree in our backyard and one day when I was nine I made my own corn pipe and smoked like a pro while I was fishing. Then I got so sick I couldn't bear it, so I've never smoked since.

Every September blackbirds used to fly into our part of Louisiana—millions of them. We'd catch them

17

and pull their heads off and give them to our mothers for blackbird stew. We weren't being cruel, we were just gathering food for survival over the winter. All winter long we'd eat blackbird stew and blackbird pie and blackbird everything else, plus cow tripe and chitlins and other items that people now call soul food. Every Sunday we'd have fried chicken—and every Sunday we kids would hope the preacher wouldn't come and eat all the good parts. Sometimes he'd come and eat everything but those scrawny old feet or the neck and the gizzard. Mom used to make us kids go stay in the kitchen while the grownups ate, but we'd peek through the crack in the door and keep track of how much the preacher was eating and which parts they were and every once in a while one of us would say, "Why don't they go home?" We always made sure we said it loud enough for the preacher to hear, but he never took the hint.

As we grew a little older we'd spend our weekend evenings at the Rescue Alley Teenage Club or Naylor's Diner Teenage Club or Pearlie's Pool Hall. We'd go to dances or to movies at the Jax Theater, but we couldn't go 24 miles over to Monroe to the movies because we didn't have a car and my mother wouldn't let me go out of Rayville anyhow.

I always obeyed my mother about not going out of Rayville and about most other things, too, and there was a good reason for my obedience. I was afraid of her. I had seen her discipline my brothers and I knew she wasn't anyone to fool around with. One time Robert was thrown into jail because he was with some friends when they were caught for stealing something earlier. Mom got him out of jail after an hour, but then I think Robert wished he'd stayed there. She took him home and strung him up to the rafter and stripped him and beat the daylights out of him while what seemed like most of the population of Rayville came into our house and pulled up chairs and watched. The pain and embarrassment were made even worse by what my mother was using—electric wire.

Dennis was whipped one time by his teacher and she hit him so hard and so often that he caught fire. He had some matches in his pocket, and that teacher was whipping him so hard she set the matches on fire—and Dennis, too.

I used to love baseball so much, though, that I was willing to take a chance on getting into trouble. We used to play on a big oat field behind my house and I'd slip out the back door when I was supposed to be doing something else and race across our backyard and jump the fence and head for the oat field. An old lady named Mrs. Menthy lived across the street from us and she had a front-porch swing and she was always in it, not missing a thing. I never did figure out how she could see me sneaking out the back door, but the minute I was out, she'd yell out from across the street in front, "Miz Savannah, he's gone again!"

Sure enough, Mom would show up at the ball field almost at the same I did, with her hands behind her back and fire in her eyes. At that moment I always had a choice to make: Let the boys see me get a whipping, or go home and get one twice as bad. My usual choice was to run home—and keep on running away from my mother around the house all day. But she always caught up with me sooner or later.

One day I was able to avoid her all day after getting caught playing baseball. Finally, late that afternoon, I was exhausted and collapsed onto my bed. I woke up a few minutes later in a blaze of electrical wire. That's the worst feeling in the world, to wake up out of a sleep and see and feel somebody whipping your hide with electrical wire as hard as they can.

I never owned a baseball glove or sneakers until

I was in high school. In fact, nobody playing baseball on the oat field owned a glove. To get a ball we had to steal one from the five-and-dime store. One guy would be picked to do the job while the rest of us would distract the store clerks. There was a security window in the middle of the store and some of the supervisors would look through there and keep an eye on us, but they never knew that while they were doing that, one of us was stealing a baseball. We became so good at it that eventually we would cluster around the candy counter and distract their attention while the hit man was stealing a ball elsewhere—and we'd be stealing candy at the same time. We were smarter than they were, and it was their store.

For all the fun I had playing it, baseball was also the source of my first few big disappointments in sports. I never made our Little League team. Every year I'd try out for it, without sneakers or glove, and every year the coaches would tell me I was a good player, but I never was picked for the team. Each player got a Little League tee shirt and I wanted one of those shirts more than anything else in the whole world, but I never did get one. So any boy or man—or girl, too, these days—who has ever made his or her Little League team has accomplished something I never could. And I wanted one of those tee shirts so badly it hurt.

Our Tom Sawyer life even had a few local legends of its own, just like in the Samuel Clemens books. There's a swamp that runs from the northern part of Louisiana down to the southern part and every year a new tale would travel up and down that swamp. The one I remember best was one summer when the town folk talked about a man 10 feet tall with one eye who was eating people up. One other time they were telling about a boy who robbed somebody and when they started to chase him his footprints turned into paw prints, so that meant he turned into a cat. Then when they trapped him in an alley, he got away and all that was found was a cat.

The stories used to spread as soon as somebody saw something which they couldn't explain. My mother even had a tale of her own. She said that every time she lit a fire she would see the old lady who used to live in our house and that the lady would come into the fire and put it out.

I experienced one of my own tales one time that almost scared the life right out of me. I had been playing with a gun that had belonged to a man who had just died. That night, while I was sleeping—in the same bed with my parents and lying between them because we had to double up and triple up—something came and slapped me. I don't know what it was or who it was, but I know I saw a man I had never seen before and he was right there in my parents' bedroom slapping me in the middle of the night. As soon as my mother heard me crying and woke up, he was gone. The next day, the gun was gone, too. My mother got that thing out of there.

One of my scariest experiences happened on a normally happy occasion. My sister Bunny was getting married. At her reception I sneaked a few swallows of champagne—which tasted awful—and then went home and ate some watermelon. A little while later I was walking down the street with a girl and all of a sudden I felt weak and it seemed that all the life was going out of me. It wasn't just my imagination. This was for real. I grabbed a light pole while everything was going dim. I was certain I was near death and I remember saying to God, "Please don't let me die." I promised to do anything He ever asked me to if He would just let me live.

Well, He did, and my brothers explained later that champagne and watermelon just don't mix, but it didn't end there. It was more than just a physical illness.

21

It was my first religious experience. I had always gone to church and Sunday school every Sunday of my life with my mother, but this was more than that. This was a moment of real closeness between.God and me.

At that moment, He saved my life. And at that same time, my life became His, not mine. I didn't know it at the time, but that's what happened, and it was all part of His divine plan, just as everything else is.

I didn't become an instant born-again Christian in the drama of the moment. I was going to church and Sunday school every week and obeying my mother about as much as any other kid that age, but my real relationship with God wasn't to come until many years later.

I know now, after making a genuine commitment to God as an adult, that I'll never turn my back on God again. That scary day in Rayville, though, the only message I received was that God was sparing my life. That message was good enough for me.

BASKETBALL:
THE TICKET
OUT

I was headed down the path of so many others by the time I was in the seventh and eighth grades. I was running with a bad crowd and getting into minor scrapes that surely would lead to more serious trouble as I grew older. That's the path to a life of working on a cotton farm and getting drunk every Saturday night and maybe winding up shot and killed. That's the way I could have gone. But I didn't, for two reasons: Reverend Calvin and basketball.

Reverend John Calvin was one of the teachers at Eulah Britton High School. He was also a Methodist minister. He knew my mother and all my aunts and uncles and he knew all my brothers and sisters who had gone through Britton ahead of me. I must have set a new Britton record for getting sent home. I was forever getting into trouble in class. One day in the eighth grade I was on my way to the office after getting kicked out of class—again—when Reverend Calvin spotted me in the hall. He went with me to the office and stuck up for me, mostly as a favor to my mother. Then he did two things that probably changed the course of my life. He arranged to have me transferred to his room, and he put me on the eighth-grade basketball team, which he coached.

He didn't do it without a warning, though. "I'm going to put your tail in my classroom," he told me, "and if you ever give me any trouble I'm going to beat you or kill you." He wouldn't have, but I got the message. Reverend Calvin drew me away from the bad crowd I had been running with. He turned me around.

The following summer I started getting some fun out of basketball. When Reverend Calvin put me on his team at school, he made me a guard because I was still on the small side. It really wasn't that much fun for me because I didn't have any idea at all of what I was doing or why I was doing it. But that summer I began to

24

acquire some of the basic skills and learn a little about the rules, so things started to make sense and added up to fun for me.

For the first time in my life, I started to play basketball instead of baseball in the summer. I was still running out the back door, hoping to escape Mrs. Menthy's eyes across the street, and jumping over our 6-foot fence instead of opening the gate, only now I wasn't headed for the oat field. Now I was headed for the basketball court.

We weren't allowed to go over to the white school and play on the outdoor court there. We had to use the one at Britton. The white school was forbidden territory for us. It was against the law for us to walk on their grass, and we'd get arrested if we ever tried to play on their basketball court, but they could come over to Britton and rip out the windows and nobody said or did anything about it. They had seven or eight baskets on their outdoor court, with real chain nets and a tin backboard and a paved playing surface. We just had one raggedy old wooden backboard nailed to an old light pole with a flimsy rim that wobbled every time a shot hit it. The wooden backboard seemed to become more warped every time it rained and our playing surface wasn't paved. It was plain old Louisiana dirt. But we played there and had more fun than you can imagine. We had only a few balls. The Ricks boys down the street had one, and Larry Ward had one—outdoor rubber balls. I never had one, but as long as one or two families could afford one that's all we needed.

I'd get up every morning that summer and shake off the rats which crawled into bed with me every night and race down to play some more basketball. By the time I was a junior in high school I was building my ability and my confidence—and I was suddenly 6 feet 2 inches tall. My mother's side of the family had finally taken over, just in time for high school.

Our high school gym was a joke, but it was home to us. It's "The Crackerbox," and it's not one bit better than the gym Bill Cosby talks about in one of his comedy routines. He and his buddies in Philadelphia weren't any worse off than we were in Louisiana. The floor was cement tile. If you were brave enough — or stupid enough—to try a layup, you went crashing into a brick wall right behind the basketball at either end. Pads? That was for sissies and rich schools. No pads for us, just that hard brick wall staring you in the face when you came driving in for that layup. It didn't bother us. We were a fast-break team and all of us were on very close terms with those walls.

You wouldn't believe how much basketball we were playing by the time I was a junior. We were in tournaments every weekend, plus our regular weekly schedule. Sometimes we'd play three or four games in one day in a weekend tournament. We'd get to the site of the tournament at eight in the morning, play a game at nine, another at twelve, another at four and the championship game—which we were always in—at eight. It all added up to 55 or 60 games a season. It also added up to a lot of stamina for me, as I became used to playing a lot of games, and almost every minute of each game, running the fast break all the time. I'm sure that's why I'm able to be among the NBA leaders every year now in minutes played and can keep on running every minute I'm in there. That's my nature, and all that playing in high school developed it.

Basketball was a maturing process for me emotionally as well as physically. I learned to endure adversity, like my deep disappointment in my junior year when we went all the way to the state finals and played the championship game over at Grambling College just 50 miles from home—and lost, to DeQuincy. I cried on the bus going home, and the knowledge that we were losing three seniors from our starting five didn't do anything to stop my tears. I didn't think we'd have nearly that good a chance to win the state championship in my senior year, so I cried some more. It was a long bus ride.

Things have a way of evening up in athletics. We fielded a team at least as good as the previous one, strong and fast with a lot of talent, including my best friend, Ronnie Jenkins. We raced our way through 53 straight wins, running up and down the cement floor of "The Crackerbox" and avoiding those brick walls at either end and winning every weekend tournament we could find all over the state.

At the end of the season, there we were, still undefeated, 53-and-0, and playing in the final game for the state championship, just like the year before. Only this time we were playing in Baton Rouge, the state capital, our opponent was DeRidder, and I was about to learn something.

The night before the championship game, after both our teams won their semi-finals, I was in a malt shop when DeRidder's center, Jessie Marshall, came in. Now I was used to seeing all types of players in those state finals—like the thirty-year-old ringers who were recalled from retirement every year to play for their old high school. But Jessie Marshall was the biggest high school player I had ever seen. He was 6 feet 8 inches tall—3 inches over me—and he weighed 230 pounds, 40 pounds on me. He was as intimidating with his mouth as he was with his size. He confronted me and threatened to blow us out the next night and shut me down. I was so scared I couldn't sleep that night.

The championship game came and Jessie Marshall picked up where his mouth left off the night before. He was scoring over me and blocking my shots and making me totally useless. Our coach finally had his fill of my performance—and Jessie's—and called time-out. He spent almost the whole 60 seconds chewing me out and demanding to know if I was going to let Jessie do that to me all night.

"You going to let him do that?" he hollered. "Are you scared of that big old boy?"

Then he slapped me in the face.

The time out ended and I took the court again, knowing I was on the spot. I decided to put my tormentor on that spot, so I started taking the game to him. I became much more aggressive than I had ever been, scoring over Jessie and around him and under him and behind him. I scored 45 points and dominated my opponent even more by grabbing more than 20 rebounds. My pants were too big and every time I went up for a shot my pants started to fall off. I spent the rest of the game shooting with my right hand and holding my pants up with my left. A few times I made a lefthanded layup to prove I could hold my pants up with either hand.

It all ended like a perfect dream. We won by more than 20 points and I was voted the tournament's most valuable player. The next day the Baton Rouge paper carried a long story about the finals and the first paragraph said something like

> Elvin Hayes scored 45 points as Eula Britton High School of Rayville defeated DeRidder for the state AA championship last night.

It was the first time my name was ever in the paper. I was so excited I was almost jumping out of my skin. I bought all the copies I could carry. Back home in Rayville, no black player ever got his name in the paper. Never, including this time.

The lesson I learned that night is still with me. I take the floor for every game confident I can beat my man and determined to do it. This feeling grew in intensity when I started playing freshman ball at the University of Houston. Don Chaney was my teammate and we were the first two black basketball players in the history of the school. We knew we couldn't just be as good as everyone else—we had to be better because we were black. I took the court for the first few games that season with a vow to destroy my opponent. And that's still my vow before every game.

Winning that state championship made me a celebrity at home, even though the papers around Rayville and Monroe never printed one line about it. It didn't make any difference. Everyone knew about it. They didn't run a story the night I scored 67 points for Britton in one game, either, but everyone found out about that, too.

The one difference it could have made was in my chances for a scholarship to college. An athlete's career success depends not only on his or her ability but on other people's knowledge of it. While Kareem Abdul-Jabbar, then playing under the name of Lew Alcindor, was getting even national attention playing for Power Memorial High School in New York and other high school stars were getting publicity in their own parts of the country, here I was scoring 67 points in one game, averaging 35, playing on a team that was to go undefeated in 54 games and win the state championship, and I couldn't get my name in the paper, not even once.

I was convinced more than ever after my junior year in high school that I just had to get out of Rayville, and a basketball scholarship was going to be my ticket. All my sisters and brothers had been salutatorians or valedictorians of their graduating classes at Britton, and

I had been on the honor roll every semester in high school and had scored the highest mark in the history of the school on our aptitude tests, but I chose basketball as my way out. It would help, though, if some of those colleges were reading about me.

Well, it turned out that they were hearing about me through their own grapevine and they didn't need newspapers. The scouts were in the stands every game I played in my senior year. It was always easy for me to know they were there. All I had to do was look up at the crowd. They were the white guys.

I was shooting every kind of shot imaginable and from every spot on the floor. I played forward, guard and center in high school, and I could hit from anywhere. So could the rest of the guys. We played 8-minute quarters and there I was scoring those 67 one night and the team topping 130 another night. I was shooting from the corners, the top of the key, all over, with jumpers and hooks and layups. Other teams tried to stop us with a zone, but it never did any good. I'd shoot them out of it.

All this time I was working by myself on what today is my trademark—my turnaround jumper. I guess I didn't really invent that shot, but I'm sure I developed it. Now the writers and announcers identify it with me. When they talk about the sky hook, they say Kareem Abdul-Jabbar. When they talk about the slam-dunk, they say Wilt Chamberlain. And when they talk about the turnaround jumper, they say Elvin Hayes.

I developed that shot because I wasn't real strong in putting up a shot when I was away from the basket. I was scoring from the outside, but I still thought I needed more power. It occurred to me to try to get up in the air and turn around at the same time and then put it up, all in one coordinated act of shooting. All summer long between my junior and senior years in high school I worked on it, every day on that dirt out-door court at Britton, always banking the shot off those tin backboards and through the crooked hoops. Gradually the coordination came, and so did new strength through my shoulders. By the time I started my senior season at Britton, I could hit on the turnaround jumper often enough that confidence was developing along with the ability.

You can't stop that shot. Everybody tries, but nobody can—not if you shoot it right. Your back is to the basket, which means your back is also to your opponent, so he can't get to the ball. Your man doesn't see the ball until you've turned around and are going up with the shot, the ball over your head. By then it's too late. The only thing they can do is foul you.

The funny thing is that after I developed that shot, I didn't really need it my last year at Britton because I had become stronger and was able to hit from anywhere on the floor. But the turnaround jumper became extremely valuable to me during my freshman year at Houston because so many of my opponents were bigger and stronger than I was. So I resorted to the turnaround jumper and kept right on scoring—zip, zip, zip—over their heads. When I was a senior at Houston I scored 62 points in one game against VMI, and I was shooting nothing but the turnaround jumper—zip, zip, zip—all night long. As a matter of fact, I became too dependent on it in college. In my early years in the NBA I forced myself to start taking other kinds of shots as well. Now I'm back to shooting from outside more than ever, from the corners and just off the circle—but the turnaround jumper is always ready whenever I want to use it, and I do—every game.

With no publicity, the college scouts still managed to find out about me and they kept sending letters to my coach, which I never saw because he didn't want me to feel the pressure. I received 75 to 100 offers of scholarships, mostly from schools in the Southeast Conference, the Southwest Conference and the Big Ten. Grambling was too close to home, and enough of my brothers and sisters had already attended Southern University, so I selected the University of Houston. It was one of the best decisions I ever made.

I disagree with the practice of college recruiters putting a great deal of pressure on high school kids. I felt entirely too much of that. Kids just shouldn't be exposed to it. I had to go to my girl friend's house out in the country for two days just to get away from the recruiters. They promised me cars, money, clothes, all those fancy things. They didn't seem to understand that what I wanted most out of college was an education.

I also disagree, emphatically, with all the pressure from coaches and even parents on a kid's college choice. The kids should be free to make that choice themselves. When I was being recruited, I felt safe as long as our season was still on. It was as if I was behind a protective glass shield and I could see all these recruiters scratching and clawing but they couldn't reach me because you can't sign a player while his season is still on. But the moment that final buzzer sounds, that protective shield vanishes and you feel like saying quickly, "I'll take you!" to the first one to reach you so you won't have to fight off all the others.

Those offers of all those other material things give high school kids the impression right away that college sports are commercial, like a business. They enter college thinking the school owes them something just because they've been recruited. But the school doesn't owe them a thing. In exchange for tuition and books, all I ever wanted from any college was an opportunity to get a good degree and play basketball in return. It was a fair and even trade.

The Houston people offered me an education and a watchful eye, promising to help me out if I ever needed it in making the adjustment. I never did, but I always knew the help was there if I needed it. At the U of H, I also knew I wouldn't have to prove anything. San Francisco offered me a scholarship, but I knew that if I went there I'd be compared to Bill Russell. The same at many other schools. That was another reason for choosing Houston. They had never had an outstanding basketball player. I wouldn't be compared to anybody.

I left Rayville, and I've never gone back to live—only for an occasional visit or over the summer after my freshman year at the U of H. I fell in love with the school and the city of Houston both. When I'd visit Rayville, it was altogether different. But I knew it wasn't changing—I was. I was seeing it as it really is, with no opportunity and nothing to do, and I could understand then why I had wanted success so badly. The people there were the finest in the world, and they still are—but Rayville was Rayville and it would never be the same for me, not the way it was during my Tom Sawyer years. It was gone, and there was no sense in trying to re-create that happiness in Rayville. It would be like looking for a penny in a muddy river. You'd never find it again.

So I headed for the University of Houston, where—just five years earlier—one of the cofounders had said, "No nigger will ever set foot on this campus."

33

THOSE
EVENTFUL
TIMES

*At the University of Houston, The Big E was destined
to be one of two central figures in a chapter of basketball
history—Houston vs. UCLA, Elvin Hayes vs. Lew
Alcindor, now Kareem Abdul-Jabbar.*

*It was E's senior year. Both teams were undefeated,
the top two teams in the nation, two giants who had
been gunning for each other for a year. There was a capacity
crown at the Astrodome—55,000 people to see a
basketball game—and a national Saturday night television
audience of 50 million. Both remain record figures
today. It was billed as the game of the century and, unlike
other events with such advanced billing, this one really
was. When it was over, the life of Elvin Hayes had taken
another turn. Just as when he left Rayville, things
would never again be the same for him. College basketball
history was made that night, and Elvin Hayes was the
one who made it.*

*Fate was giving Elvin a rare opportunity in that
game against UCLA, but fate was also not above
throwing a few obstacles in his way, starting with his first
day in college.*

Two years after James Meredith's enrollment at the
University of Mississippi touched off a shooting war
there and only one year after Governor George Wallace
stood in the doorway to the University of Alabama and
swore no black would ever go to that school, Don
Chaney and I integrated the basketball program at the
University of Houston.

Don's career with the Celtics and Lakers and
mine with the Rockets and Bullets seemed a long way
off, but if anyone had to break the color line in U of H
basketball, maybe Don and I were the best choices fate
could have made. We were in a Southern city, with typical prejudices, it was the mid-1960's, with all the racial

unrest of those years making headlines all over the country—stories about demonstrations and freedom riders and the March on Washington with Martin Luther King, Jr., and the race riots in Watts and Detroit and other places, and the fiery language of people like Stokley Carmichael and Rap Brown. It was an uneasy time.

Houston, both the school and the city, wasn't violent, but the prejudice was there in subtle and effective ways. You'd go into a restaurant—they'd let you in with no argument—and never be served. You'd go into a store and never get waited on. And as the first few black students began to enroll at the University, some of the instructors were saying, "They may come here, but they'll never pass any of my courses."

Maybe fate knew what it was doing when it fingered Don and me to break the basketball color barrier there. We were a couple of black kids who had grown up in the South. Don was from near Baton Rouge and we had played against each other in tournaments and had become good friends. We were recruited together by the U of H and shown around the campus and the town on the same weekend. My fondness for him was one of my main reasons in picking Houston as my school. We both knew what we were getting into, but we had endured racial prejudice before and were confident we could do it again while breaking down some old barriers.

Loyola University of Chicago, the University of Cincinnati and the University of Oklahoma won't play the University of Houston now because of the way their black players were treated in Houston. They had to stay in the private homes of Houston's black citizens instead of in the team's hotel. They were mistreated in other ways as well. And when Oklahoma came to Houston with four blacks on its starting five, the Sooners were greeted on the court by signs criticizing their "niggers" and one white fan spent the entire game just screaming "nigger! nigger! nigger!" at the top of his lungs. Eventually the same things happened to us. We were playing one night against Jacksonville Junior College in Texas when I heard a little boy in the stands say to his mother, "Mommy! Mommy! Look at the niggers!"

If Oklahoma's black players were anything like Don and me, yelling "nigger" at them wouldn't have any effect at all. Shoot, white people had been calling us that all our lives.

Don and I had never played against a white team or even a white player until we got to Houston. One guy guarding me in our freshman year kept calling me a nigger the whole game, and would talk about my mother and call her a "mammy." He didn't make me mad, just more determined. He didn't know it, but I was immune to that sort of thing by then. I didn't even bother to answer him. I just kept playing and scoring and he kept hollering insults and getting more frustrated every time I scored. But to show you how things can turn around, that same guy transferred to Houston and played varsity ball with me. When that happened, our coach, Guy Lewis, called me aside to make sure I didn't have any hard feelings left over from our freshman game. I told him, "Shoot, no, Coach. What's new about name-calling?"

I was determined, with a fire burning inside me, to prove myself against all those white players—teammates and opponents alike. They were getting a free ride compared to Chaney and me. They were white and accepted and talented. We were talented but not much else when we started. We had to be great on the court and behave ourselves off it. We were in the same kind of situation Jackie Robinson found himself in when he became the first black man to play major league baseball.

On a smaller scale, of course, but a similar situation. The pressure was on us.

That was when the competitive fire in me was ignited. At the start of each game in that freshman year, I'd look at my opponent and say to myself, "I'm going to destroy you. Whatever you try to do to score, I'm going to be right there with you. And when I have the ball, I'm going to come right at you."

To make my mission even harder, I was going up against bigger guys. I was 6-5 at this point, and I was playing against guys 6-8 and 6-9. They weighed 245 pounds, 35 pounds more than I did. But I wasn't going to back down, and I never did.

I almost didn't get to play college basketball, and I wonder sometimes what my life would have been if my first day on the Houston campus had been a little worse than it was.

I had just checked into my room in the athletic dorm. Classes wouldn't start for another couple of days. Some of the guys I was meeting for the first time suggested we play some basketball outside. One of the guys who went along apparently was taking an immediate dislike to me. I don't know whether it was for racial reasons or whatever, but he simply refused to have anything to do with me that afternoon. He ignored me and wouldn't speak.

Late in the game I was driving for a layup against this guy and I went up to dunk the ball. He hit me hard across the back of my hand and broke it, my shooting hand. I couldn't do anything with it for six weeks. It was the first time I had ever been injured playing basketball, and I'm sure it was an accident, but if it had been any worse on that cement outdoor court, I might never have played another game.

An even closer call came the next year. It was a

stupid thing, the kind of thing college kids do, and it almost killed me.

I was horsing around in the dorm with my roommate, Howie Lorch, and a few others when Howie and I started chasing each other. I was running from Howie when I ran right through a glass door and out into the hall. I whipped around and all the guys were looking at me in complete astonishment, but all I was doing was standing there and laughing and saying, "You can't catch me, Howie, you can't catch me."

I didn't know what I was saying or doing, and to this day I don't remember those first few minutes after I went through the door. I was on my feet but only semiconscious, I had cuts in my head and my right wrist—my shooting hand again. The episode permanently damaged the nerves in my right thumb and some of the fingers of my right hand. Even today I feel tinges occasionally when I'm shooting. There were two lucky things about that incident: 1) the season had just ended, and 2) I didn't get killed.

Coach Lewis immediately ordered no more horsing around in the athletic dorm. That ended the horseplay, but it didn't end the effects of my injury. Until two years ago I was still picking bits of glass out of my forehead.

Gary Phillips had graduated from Houston and was trying to make it in the NBA with San Francisco when I was a freshman. One day I walked into our athletic dorm just in time to hear the white players talking about Gary. One of them said, "Gary would be starting if it weren't for that nigger."

Then they noticed me and fell all over themselves apologizing, but it didn't make any difference to me. They were talking about Al Attles and their choice of words was something I was used to. I didn't like the word and still don't, but after hearing it

40

from the day I was born, I could shrug it off. If I had let it get to me every time I heard the word, I would have gone nuts at an early age.

A lot of the credit for integrating Houston's sports program really belongs not to Don and me but to our coach, Guy Lewis, and his assistant, Harvey Pate. They were like fathers to us, showing us respect and treating every one of us the same—black or white. They didn't promise anything special to Chaney and me when we started playing there. Instead, Coach Lewis made sure to tell us we would not get any special treatment, but neither would the whites. He said we'd have to earn a job, and the only promise he made was to work our tails off. He kept his promise.

Guy Lewis made me the player I am, by being the kind of coach he is. He and his wife would invite me to their house and entertain me and feed me. During the summer they'd drive me from Houston to Rayville at the start of their own vacation, and I'd sit in the back seat and play games with their kids.

On the court, Coach Lewis was a taskmaster, working on me constantly to help both my offense and my defense. When he was working me too hard or getting too tough with me, I'd give him a hurt look and say, "You just don't like black players." He would get all upset at that and deny it several different ways and I'd stand there laughing but still unable to convince him I was only kidding.

All through my first two years, my roommate, Howie Lorch, was swearing he was going to make me an All-American. All-American! The idea staggered me, but Howie kept promising me he'd make it happen. He never did explain how an equipment manager could make a player an All-American.

Besides, that job belonged to Ted Nance, Houston's sports publicity director. I don't know how it happened, but after my sophomore year—freshmen weren't eligible to play varsity ball those days—I was voted to several All-American teams. Thanks to Ted, I repeated my junior and senior years. With his help, I joined Wilt Chamberlain, Jerry Lucas and Oscar Robertson as the only players to make All-American every year they were eligible. Kareem Abdul-Jabbar did it right after me the next year, and Pete Maravich has since made it, too.

Howie and I were very close, even for room-mates. He was white, 5-8, from Schenectady, New York, and over the years we formed sort of a Gale Sayers-Brian Piccolo relationship. We're still close and we see each other during the off-season in Houston, where he's a stockbroker. Howie guided me around the campus during my early months. He advised me to concentrate on speech courses instead of American history, which I favored, because he said he couldn't understand me and nobody else could, either. He coached me on how to talk and act during radio and television interviews—and he kept the cakes coming from his parents' bakery back home.

Howie was good for my appetite in other ways, too. On my twentieth birthday, he took me out to din-ner. Like any good ol' Southern boy, I picked a fried chicken place, but I did it for another reason, too: I wanted to take it easy on Howie's wallet. So I chose one of those places where you can get a bucket of nine pieces, supposedly enough for three people, but that's only if they're content with three pieces each. I ate two buckets.

On another night, Howie found out about a pan-cake house that was running a special—all you can eat for 44 cents. You got four pancakes per serving. About halfway through my meal they started bringing me two

42

servings at a time. I finished with eleven servings—44 pancakes.

By the time I was eating my last couple of servings, people were standing around watching me. And Howie was loving every minute of it. He used to tell people, "That was one of his best nights. That's when he's at his best, after six. He can't go to sleep on an empty stomach." We went back a week later. The special had been discontinued.

My reputation with a knife and fork was beginning to get around. I was asked about it even in a television interview. The reporter said, "What's your favorite dish?"

I said, "Pork chops."

"How many can you eat?"

"Man, I don't count them. I just eat them."

That first year was a time of adjustment, and some of my friends back home never did give me much of a vote of confidence. When I left home they told me, "You ain't gonna amount to nothin'." They told me I'd be swallowed up by the bigness of Houston and the competition and I'd drop out and be back in Rayville in no time.

But I never for one minute doubted that I'd make it. I didn't have any wild ideas about being an All-American, and I certainly never wasted my time dreaming about being voted College Player of the Year, but I knew for sure that I was going to play varsity basketball and get myself a good education and make good at something.

I had made a business deal with the university—my basketball for their knowledge. Some guys who don't make it in the NBA and didn't have the good sense to get an education while they were in college go around complaining that their school took advantage of them. I don't buy that. It's a deal, and the school will get theirs. You'll play basketball for them, so they'll collect their half of the trade. If you don't collect your half, that's your fault, not theirs. When you agree to the trade by accepting their scholarship, the school doesn't guarantee you an education. They merely guarantee you the *opportunity* for one. I was aware of the difference.

I didn't know what profession I would follow, and it was too soon to think about pro basketball, but I was going to get an education no matter what. But I was almost done in my own poor study habits, a carryover from high school when I didn't have to study hard to get good grades. At Houston, two hours a night are set aside in the athletic dorm for studying, and the coaches make you stay in your room. This was all year long. You couldn't even be found in the hall without being questioned.

Howie would hit the books, but in my freshman year my high school experiences made me think I didn't have to do any homework. I'd go nuts with boredom without anyone to talk to while Howie was slaving over his studies. Gradually, with his encouragement, I saw the light and developed good study habits.

I don't go around giving a whole lot of advice, but I will say that any athlete entering college better have good study habits or develop them fast. If you don't, you're going to face two possibilities—you'll be declared ineligible for athletics or you'll flunk out.

In my first speech course, I wasn't sure I was going to get an education at all. The instructor, who should have been retired by that time and was later, was a lover of Edgar Allan Poe's works. Anytime a student started to recite Poe in her class, she'd jump up and yell, "No! No! No one is allowed to recite Poe but me!"

Every day for that whole first semester, she made us start the class by reciting one of the all-time greats:

Twinkle, twinkle, little star.
How I wonder what you are.
Up above the world so high
Like a diamond in the sky.

It was intended to help our expression and elocution, but I grew so bored with that class I'd start talking to the girl next to me, and we'd both get kicked out of class. Always the message was the same: "Mr. Hayes, if you were a true Southern gentleman, you would not be talking in class. You are excused."

For our final exam, we had to recite—individually—guess what: Twinkle, twinkle, little star. And so on and on and on.

They had a lot of excellent teachers at Houston while I was there, competent people who helped me a lot. She just didn't happen to be one of them.

I thank the Good Lord I was able to go to college, and that He gave me the good sense to recognize the opportunity and make the most of it. Not only did I get a good education and improve myself as a person, I had a lot of good times. It's too bad not all young people have this chance, but those who do certainly shouldn't miss both opportunities, a good education and a good time.

I never would have thought about applying as a hardship case so I could play pro basketball before my college class graduated, even if I had been able. Every player should finish college if at all possible. I wouldn't trade those four years for anything. I'm not even sure the hardship rule is a good thing. I think the NBA should consider dropping it, and a lot of other NBA players and coaches feel the same way.

There's no guarantee you'll make it in the pros, even after graduation, and your chances are naturally reduced if you're a year or two younger. If you do make it, there's still no guarantee you'll play. Darryl Dawkins for Philadelphia, for example, sat on the end of the bench in the pros when he could have been playing regularly in college, developing his basketball skills and body, getting an education for the day when he won't be a basketball player anymore, and having fun at the same time. He's a typical case. You don't have any fun on the bench, even in the pros.

That's why I think maybe the hardship rule should be dropped. It's no advantage at all. It hurts young players in the long run instead of helping them.

I picked up more than an education and a profession at Houston. I picked up my nickname, too. John Hollis was covering the Cougars for the *Houston Post* and, as fate would have it, he had been in the Navy and assigned to the giant aircraft carrier, the *U.S.S. Enterprise,* whose nickname is "The Big E." He wrote that I destroyed the enemy the same way the *Enterprise* does, that I was The Big E of college basketball. That was more than ten years ago. I went on to the NBA, John went on to become sports editor of the *Post,* and the nickname stuck.

I've always liked the name, and in its own way it's helped to establish me as a basketball figure. Even something like that name is another case of how lucky I've always considered myself. If I hadn't been covered by someone who had been stationed on the *Enterprise,* the nickname may never have been born—or if my parents hadn't given me a name starting with E. There's a story there, too.

All of us kids were named after relatives. By the time they got to me, the baby of the family of six children, they were running out of possibilities, so they named me after an aunt, my father's sister, Elvin. It's a name that's been in the family for several generations, but never given to a boy until they hit a generation that ran out of boys' names. So I might never have become The Big E if that hadn't happened—and they hadn't given me a girl's name.

I never took part in any of the anti-war demonstrations or race protests which were so common while I was in college in the mid-1960's, and I certainly would never have anything to do with a riot of any kind because I don't believe in violence, regardless of the cause. There were a lot of changes in the making in Houston the city and at Houston the university, but the people and the government officials were able to keep the lid on things while making progress on the changes people were trying to make.

The school administration by now was developing a much more progressive attitude toward blacks, and if enough of us wanted a black history course, we'd go to the administration and ask and they'd give us one. The school's officials were always cooperative, much more than you might have expected at that time in a Southern city. Generally, you got what you asked for—if it was reasonable and valid—and most blacks had confidence in the system.

But there was a lot of dissatisfaction on campus about the war in Vietnam. The Gulf of Tonkin incident that led to the American military buildup over there happened in my freshman year, 1964, and the year I graduated, 1968, was the year of the Tet offensive by the North Vietnamese and the riots at the Democratic convention in Chicago, and the fall from power of one of our fellow Texans, Lyndon Johnson. So that four-year span of my college career also covered the first four bitter and hot years of the war protest movement on America's college campuses.

The reason I never joined in any of the protests, though, was that I could identify with both sides and I understood the thinking on both sides. I was a college student, and I knew how the students felt in their intense objections to the war. We were being asked to go to a war many didn't understand and risk getting killed for a cause that many didn't agree with.

But that never did justify violence and bloodshed to protest violence and bloodshed. And I could see the other side's view anyhow. My brother Dennis had been in the Navy all his adult life, and my sister Bunny's husband was a captain in the Army, so I had been exposed to the career military man by the time I entered college and could understand their attitudes. They were both in Vietnam while I was at the U of H. Dennis was on a supply boat, one of those small ships running up those narrow rivers and shallow canals that we used to see on the evening television news. And Al was over there in combat fighting the Vietcong.

With my own family members over there in that kind of dangerous duty, I could hardly take to the streets and protest in violent disagreement with what they were doing. It was an angry time and some people seemed to lose their sense of direction, but that made it even more important for the rest of us to keep ours. That's why I would never have told anyone to go or not go. You had to try to keep your cool in those days and honestly try to find out what was right and look into your heart and soul for a long time, then go ahead and do what you thought you should.

I don't believe in defiance and disobedience and death just because you disagree with someone. That's no better than what the drunks used to do in Rayville on Saturday night. I believed, and still do, that you work within the system. Things like obedience and loyalty are words you didn't hear very often in those days, but I was still playing the game that way, and I do today.

I didn't burn down the building when I received

my notice to register for the draft. I just went. I walked into the draft board's office in Rayville and I was scared, but the law said I had to do this, so I was doing it. I was a junior at Houston by this time, 6 feet 9 inches tall. Every inch of me was scared until the lady said, "You don't ever have to worry about being drafted. You're too tall. You can go on home now."

I left that place with a smile all over my face. I was never so glad to be so tall.

But if that hadn't happened, and they had ordered me to report for the draft, I would have gone. And if they had sent me to Vietnam, I would have gone there, too. I believe in America, so I would have gone. Some people disagree with that, and at college some of my classmates used to try to argue me out of that attitude. Some blacks were saying in those days that I shouldn't feel that way, not just because of the war but because of racial discrimination, too.

But I'm from America. I'm not from Africa. My ancestors may have been born in Africa, but I was born here. There is no country in the world greater than America. I've traveled all over the world and I think I know what I'm talking about when I say that no nation in the world offers more freedom to its citizens, or greater opportunity to everyone, than America does. We've made our mistakes, some of them recently, but that doesn't shake my belief in America or my love for it.

Nobody has to teach me about prejudice and poverty and discrimination. I grew up with all that. I know it's here, and I know it a lot better than some of the people who go around preaching about it and saying how awful it is. Sure it's awful. Sure it's wrong. But it's no worse here than anywhere else, and in fact it's a lot better here than anywhere else. And there's one other point that people tend to overlook: In America, the *opportunity* is always there. Maybe I would have a different attitude if America didn't offer its people opportunity, but it does. I took advantage of that, and other people can, too. So how could I feel any other way about this country?

THE
BIGGEST
GAME
IN COLLEGE
BASKETBALL
HISTORY

While Elvin Hayes was enjoying life as an All-American athlete and college student, events were unfolding which were to lead to one of the most dramatic contests in the history of college sports.

With The Big E leading the way, Houston's Cougars reached new heights, the semi-finals of the National Collegiate Athletic Championship, against the mighty UCLA Bruins. There was to be no magic Cinderella story that day in March 1967 in Louisville, and UCLA defeated the Cougars.

Immediately the speculation began to build. What would happen next year? The two teams were to meet as part of their regular season's schedule. Would UCLA, undefeated for over a year that day in Louisville, still be undefeated almost a year later, on a January night in Houston? Would Houston be one of the top teams in the country the night of the rematch? Would Elvin Hayes and Lew Alcindor dominate college basketball even more the next season, and thus face each other in a classic individual duel while their teams were also slugging it out?

If the answers to all these questions came up yes, surely it would be the greatest basketball game in college basketball history. It happened.

Ted Nance wasn't taking any chances. With his eye on that schedule for the next season, Nance, the Houston PR director, began beating the drum right after the loss to UCLA in March of 1967. He was ballyhooing it for almost a year as the greatest college game ever, and as the events continued to unfold, no one was arguing with him.

The UCLA powerhouse rolled on, 47 straight victories, not one loss in two years. The Cougars picked right up at the start of that 1967–68 season, trying to forget the UCLA loss but still swearing revenge, all the while avoiding the trap of overlooking their immediate opponent.

*Everyone associated with the Houston team
knew it was essential to be undefeated going into the UCLA
game so as to preserve its classic dimensions. But they
also knew that every one of the sixteen teams before the
UCLA spot on the schedule would be gunning for the
Cougars, determined to be the team that spoiled the season
for Houston even before UCLA got the chance.*

*One such scare came in the Hawaii Rainbow
Classic over the Christmas Holidays. Houston was losing to
North Texas State by something like 20 points at the
half. State was playing a deliberate style of offense, thus
choking off Houston's famed fast break. Then, for
reasons unknown to Houston, State came out running in the
second half. Houston won easily.*

*All the pieces of the drama were now in place,
UCLA with its 47 straight, Houston now 16-0, Alcindor
and Hayes poised for each other, and 52,693 paying
fans and a few thousand guests gathered in the Houston
Astrodome for the first basketball game ever played
there. Many of the fans held binoculars in the cavernous
arena.*

*It was the largest crowd ever to see a college
basketball game, topped only by the 75,000 who saw the
Harlem Globetrotters in Berlin. But those numbers were
dwarfed by the size of the television audience—some 55
million, the largest number of people ever to see a college
basketball game.*

*Fate had held things together neatly since that game
ten months earlier in Louisville, and now that throng
in the Astrodome and the far larger audience in front of
America's TV sets that Saturday night, January 20,
1968, prepared for what they knew was a classic matchup. It
was Dempsey vs. Tunney, the Yankees vs. the Dodgers,
Jack Nicklaus vs. Gary Player, Billy Jean King vs. Chris
Evert, the Raiders vs. the Vikings, Muhammed Ali vs.
Joe Frazier.*

53

*Down there in the center of the floor, in this stadium
built for football and baseball and their huge crowds,
playing on what looked to one writer like a postage stamp,
were the two leading characters in this classic duel.
Elvin Hayes and Lew Alcindor crouched, eyes zeroed in on
the ball held aloft by the referee.
Elvin Hayes remembers how it felt.*

The atmosphere was telling us, "This is it. All the practices, all the publicity, all the buildup, it's all come down to these forty minutes. It's all here. It's all before you."

And yet, I don't think there was any nervousness. The confidence was there. I had never seen the guys like this. There wasn't a lot of talking in the dressing room or out on the floor during the warmups. There wasn't a lot of jiving around. We used to bring a record player into the dressing room and play the top sounds before every game and we'd dance around and do a lot of clowning. We'd really get loose. And we always played "Sweet Georgia Brown," just like the Globetrotters, before taking the floor.

It was the same this night with one big difference. I noticed there wasn't any dancing around. The music was there, as always. But there was no dancing around. Instead of dancing there was concentration. Everyone was preparing himself for his assignments on offense and defense, just mentally reviewing what he had to do. When we left the locker room, we left in silence—not the silence of defeatism or fear but the silence of concentration. We wanted this, and we weren't fooling around about it.

As we walked down the ramp from the dressing room to the court, we could hear the high-level buzz of the huge crowd. UCLA was already on the floor warming up. As we came into the view of the crowd, a roar

54

sounding like an explosion erupted and engulfed us. We were surrounded by sound, the happy sound of what has come to be known as "the home-court advantage."

The crowd just went nuts. That's the only way to describe it. I think the fans were more nervous than we were. With us players, there was no more nervousness, no more doubt. We just *knew* we were going to win. The enthusiasm among us was incredible. I had never seen us so united and caring for one another the way I sensed we were caring for one another this night. With that feeling, the moment we hit the floor I felt I could jump to the sky.

I couldn't wait for the game to start. Usually in pre-game warmups, I'll shoot from all over, usually taking a lot of shots. But tonight I was taking only a few outside shots and nothing inside. I just kept walking around, walking around. The team huddled and then waited for the introductions. The public-address announcer was wasting his breath. Nobody could hear any Houston name. We would just look at each other and point to ourselves and say, "My turn?" One by one we ran to the center of the court and the crowd just kept right on screaming as each of us ran out.

I was the last one introduced. Before I even started to run out, the crowd was on its feet and screaming in what sounded like one high-pitched, piercing siren: "E! E! E!" Now I was more anxious than ever, but I still had the national anthem to wait through. I love the national anthem because I love America, but this night I wanted it to be the quickest version ever played. All I could think was, "Let me get out there. Let me at them."

Our strategy was to keep UCLA spread out in a zone defense. One of my jobs was to take Kareem (Alcindor) away from the basket and away from his spot on the floor. We kept collapsing on him on defense and sealing off any options he might have had for going to anyone else. On offense, a big part of the load would have to be carried by our point guard, George Reynolds. George was the greatest point guard I've ever played with. He knew exactly what each player could do, where his best shots were, and he was a good shooter himself. He was absolutely one of the most unselfish players I've ever had the pleasure of playing with. I wanted to put him in my pocket and take him into the pros with me. If you were open at ten feet but he knew you were better at five feet, he'd get the ball to you at five feet. That's how good he was. Tonight he'd need every bit of that ability if we were to win.

All these things were going through my mind, and every other player's on the Houston team, when Kareem and I waited to jump to start the game. The ref flipped the ball into the air. We both went up. I got the tip and hit it over to Don Chaney. He passed to George and George got the ball to me near the lane. I went up with the first shot of the game, a turnaround jumper. It was good. Then we stole the ball and I came right at Kareem with a hook shot from the foul line. It was good, too—4-0. The crowd was out of its mind, but we had to keep our cool.

We got the ball back and George hit me for a shot over Kareem from the foul line—6-0. UCLA had Edgar Lacey and then Mike Lynn guarding me, with Kareem helping out, but I was able to keep right on scoring. I had 16 points in the first 10½ minutes.

On defense our strategy was working. Ken Spain and I were keeping Kareem away from the basket and shutting off his options. Lucius Allen was their only offense. He was forced to create things out there, free-lancing, because we had taken away their offense.

We were ahead by as much as 15 at one point,

and at the half we led, 46–43. I had taken 19 shots and made 14 of them. We were really smoking. In the dressing room at halftime, Coach Lewis told us the only thing we had to do was to maintain our attitude of concentration and confidence. He did a great job of making sure we did, while he kept our fire burning.

UCLA didn't back off. John Wooden must have done as good a job of talking to his team at the half as Coach Lewis did, because the Bruins came right at us at the start of the second half. They made up that 3-point deficit and caught up with us, 54–54. We went ahead again and they caught us again, 65–65, with three minutes and two seconds left in the game.

Theodis Lee hit me with a pass at the baseline and I scored and Don Chaney hit from 18 feet to make it 69–65 with 1:57 left. But UCLA, like a true champion, refused to go down. Lucius Allen made a layup and then came back with two free-throws a few seconds later and it was tied again, 69–69. There were 44 seconds left.

The fans knew they were seeing a game for the history books, one every bit as good as the buildup had predicted. The players were aware of it, too. We knew we were taking part in one of the greatest games ever played, and not just because of all the ingredients going into it. It was turning out to be one of the best-played games ever as well—with excellent scoring, defense, rebounding. I don't think there has ever been such a fundamentally sound game, by both teams. Every pass was just what a coach would want—crisp, quick, right on the money. On every rebound, the men underneath were getting position, blocking out. The shooters were not only making their shots, they were showing good shot selection and perfect form with their rhythm and followthrough. On defense, the men were taking textbook positions with picture-perfect stances and turn-ins. Both teams were executing the fast break the way you see it in those instructional films. The ball-handling and play-calling by the guards was almost perfect.

The whole game was being played that way, the greatest game was being played as the perfect game.

The two greatest teams of the year were slugging it out, back and forth, the way two great opponents are expected to. So now it was 69—69. We were down to half a minute when I got the ball down low on the left side. I was turning to the corner, starting my turn-around jumper, when I was fouled by Jim Nielsen. There were 28 seconds left.

I was about a 60 percent free-throw shooter that year, and some people used to say I wasn't very good at it. I never could understand that. Here I was smashing scoring records all over the place for three years and I'm getting criticized by some as supposedly a poor foul shooter. So I guess I had more confidence than some of the people in that crowd as I stepped to the foul line.

I accepted the ball from the ref and looked at the basket. The crowd was so quiet it was almost as if they weren't there. I knew they were all scared stiff. But I had a clear and relaxed mind. I didn't even think about being nervous. I made the first shot. We had the lead again, 70–69. But one point wasn't enough. We needed 2 so a basket by UCLA wouldn't defeat us. We needed a 2-point lead and we needed to maintain it for the longest 28 seconds of our lives.

We got it. My second shot was good. Now we had to hold them off, don't give them anything easy. No fouls. No 3-point play. By all means, no 3-point play. If they score, they still have only a tie, and we have the ball and a chance to score at the buzzer—unless UCLA plays for one last shot to send it into overtime.

We put on a full-court press. Then the unexpected. UCLA's inbound pass hit one of its own players and went out of bounds. I caught our own inbound pass

58

and ran down the clock. Normally I would have looked to George Reynolds to pass to him so he could handle the ball, but I was so confident by this time I was sure I could do anything, so I decided to act like a point guard myself for a few seconds. With four seconds left, I passed to George. Then the buzzer sounded. It was all over. We had defeated the champions. It was Christmas morning, Graduation Day, the Fourth of July and everything else all in one. And a giant weight was suddenly lifted from my shoulders and I could explode with both joy and relief. I jumped straight up and ran toward George. He was doing the same thing and heading for me. We met at halfcourt and hugged each other like two sweethearts, or like that famous picture of Yogi Berra hugging Don Larsen after Larsen's perfect game in the World Series.

The crowd poured onto the postage-stamp floor, and then they did something nice. They carried me off on their shoulders.

It was a game which was to change the life of Elvin Hayes permanently. He was a national celebrity now. The phone wouldn't stop ringing with requests for interviews. The pro scouts were on his trail hotter than ever. He was the toast of the campus and of the entire city. And this young college student, who never saw his name in the paper in high school, saw both his name and his picture on the cover of Sports Illustrated.

It's funny how different people act in different ways. After that game, I went over to Kareem's hotel and congratulated him on a good game. Then several of the Houston players took him to one of their own fraternity parties. It was just the kind of atmosphere which should prevail after a game, no matter who wins or loses. Kareem was great in defeat, and that's one of the reasons I like him and respect him. He's just a very nice person. And we were trying to be the same way, trying to be good winners.

But not everyone felt that way after that game. Some of the other UCLA players were bitter and said some things that didn't reflect much credit on them or their school. And even today, a couple of those guys are still angry about that defeat.

That's hard to believe, but it's true. I know it.

And some of the press started writing a convenient alibi for UCLA—that Kareem had injured his eye a few games earlier and wasn't at his best, that he was having trouble seeing. If he was having trouble seeing, how come he was nine-for-nine from the free-throw line? They said he had double vision, and my answer to that was the only double vision he was having was Ken Spain and me going up in his face every time he tried a shot.

But Kareem—Lew Alcindor—was a champion after they lost to us in the Astrodome. He has always been a nice guy, and he was before the game and after, too. I respect him both as a great athlete and as a great person. After the game, he was the same as ever, no sour attitude because he lost—and in his case, a poor attitude might have been understandable. He was playing in a losing basketball game for only the second time in his life. His high school team in New York—Power Memorial High—lost only one game, to De Matha High School outside Washington, D.C. And his UCLA teams had all been undefeated. But he didn't let this unusual experience bother him. He knew that one reason they lost was because he just didn't get to take that many good shots. The films show it. It was one of those nights

60

when a particular team just seemed to be picked by destiny to win. That night it happened to be Houston.

That may be some of the Elvin Hayes modesty showing.
If destiny won the game for Houston, then The Big E helped
destiny get her way. He completely outperformed
Alcindor, outscoring him 39 to 15. He hit on 17 of 25 field-
goal attempts and five of seven free- throws. He
grabbed off 15 rebounds to Alcindor's 12, had four assists on
baskets and topped off his championship performance by
blocking eight shots.

It seemed significant, even appropriate, that he
scored the Cougars' first points, the ones that got them
started, and their last points, the ones that delivered the
victory.

It's impossible to describe how relieved I felt after that game. I had been under sustained pressure for months and months. I had to make All-American for the third time, we had to win every game leading up to UCLA, we had to win that one game which we had been preparing for over a whole year, I had to maintain good grades in college, I had to be able to hold up under continuing national publicity and all the interviews and personal appearances which that involves, and people wanted me to beat out Kareem and be voted College Player of the Year—all this and I was still only 22 years old.

It really gets to you at times, and it got to me. People say, "Look at Elvin Hayes. He's cool. Never lets the pressure bother him. Nothing ever fazes him." Well, that's not true, and if you think about it, how could it be? Any athlete is only a human being like the fans in the stands and the writers in the press box. A lot of times the burden of trying to be a great athlete comes more from the outside pressures than from what you're trying to do on the court or on the field. In the case of college athletes, even more so. There's the added pressure of having to maintain your grades if you are to remain scholastically eligible to play athletics. You have to find time to do homework after attending class and practicing for three hours every day. On the road you have your homework to do and you have to be as ready for that next class when you get back after two weeks of travel as the students who have been attending every class while you've been gone.

In our case, a whole city was expecting us to be the No. 1 team in the nation, and every opponent was climbing up our mountain and trying to knock us off. And as if all this weren't enough, I had to worry about taking care of my wife and our new son.

I couldn't get away from the pressure. I couldn't just go home. At times I would want to stay in bed, but I knew I couldn't do that, either. And as a senior, I had my whole adult life getting closer every day. I knew the world was saying, "Before long you'll be mine." There would be no break for me. And because I was living with my family in an apartment and not in the athletic dorm, there was no coach to come around every morning and say, "Get out of bed so you can stay in school." And there was no coach to come around at night during those two hours of study and make sure I was in my room and hitting the books.

It was all on my shoulders, all the basketball pressures, the family pressures, the scholastic pressures. It was even more difficult in my case, not just because I was always in the national spotlight, but also because I had not really been prepared by my earlier years for all these pressures. I'm not sure any kid 21 could really have been made ready in those few years to cope with the amount of pressure I was carrying, but it was even harder for me because I was from a pressure-free background. I was from a small town that had been ignored by the white press. Everything seemed much more relaxed back in Rayville.

Now, here I was carrying this load, and it was difficult—very difficult. I didn't have a father to turn to. I didn't know what to do. Erna was busy with little Elvin and her own college studies, so I didn't want to add to her burden. I felt very alone. At times in college I would feel anger and frustration, but I tried to hold myself in check. Every time I had the opportunity, I would sneak away to a small bayou across the school from the campus in MacGregor Park. I'd go there and lie on the grass and ask myself, "God, how long can all this last? I can't wait to get away from it all."

The fans and the writers see some big star out there getting a lot of attention and recognition and, if he or she is a pro, a lot of money, but they have no way of knowing how much of a load that athlete might be carrying. Someone who looks as if he has the world on a string might be feeling pressures which are almost unbearable. That's the kind of feeling that would come over me often in my senior year, and I would slip away to the bayou across the street at every chance and lie on the ground and try to regain control of myself, like refilling your car's gas tank, and I would marvel at what a difference there was between one side of Cullen Boulevard and the other.

On that historic night when his team beat the unbeatable, when the University of Houston and Elvin Hayes crashed onto the national scene at the expense of UCLA and Lew Alcindor, The Big E was playing under additional burdens which the public knew nothing about.

His mother, brothers and sisters, nephews and cousins and teachers all had made the trip from Rayville for the big game. Erna and Elvin found themselves running a hotel and a taxi service before and after the game. Elvin jokes today that with all the running around to pick up visiting relatives from the airport, he almost didn't have time to show up for the game. On game day, he didn't even have time for a nap. "I thought I was going to have a horrible game," he remembers today. And so, unknown to press and public alike, Elvin Hayes showed up for his role in that classic battle needing a good rest.

After the game, when exhaustion would have overtaken a lesser man, Elvin Hayes stayed at the Astrodome and remained on his feet for another two hours, signing autographs without complaint.

WELCOME TO THE NBA

That senior year was the hardest, although the most successful, of my life to that point, and I'm sure there was a connection between the burdens I was feeling and the successes I was achieving. I know success never comes easy, and after that year, nobody had to tell me about it. But the burdens were nothing compared to what lay ahead of me, two years later, beginning with the second season of my professional career, the after-effects of which follow me to this day.

None of that was on the horizon, though, when I began my NBA career with the San Diego Rockets. Everything was coming up roses. The Rockets' owner, Bob Breitbard, had followed my senior year closely. Three days after we lost to UCLA in the NCAA semifinals and we played a useless consolation game which we lost to Ohio State—all consolation games are a waste of everybody's time—I flew with Erna and a few others to San Diego. Mr. Breitbard said he wanted to handle the negotiations with me himself, without the general manager. Sometimes an owner will do that, and it's his privilege. He's the owner. I felt flattered and he gave me a great deal, but it was one of the things that came back to haunt me two years later.

I wasn't going to play cat-and-mouse with Mr. Breitbard. I was being recruited by the Houston Mavericks of the American Basketball Association, who wanted me because of my hometown popularity and the help that would give them at the gate. I knew I was in a favorable bargaining position, and Mr. Breitbard knew it, too. I didn't want any prolonged period when we would be playing games with each other in the papers, and the Mavericks would be hot after me and I'd have to put up with all that recruiting nonsense that I got after high school. I just wasn't going through that again.

The Mavericks were telling Don Chaney and me how much they wanted both of us, and I'm sure they

66

did. The ABA was trying to survive in its war with the NBA. They'd invite me to their practices and take me out to dinner during my senior year, being careful not to talk business and jeopardize my eligibility. Then when they found out I was in San Diego talking contract with the Rockets, they became panicky and called me and started talking big money, but they never came up with any. Besides, I wanted to play in the NBA. I wanted to compete against the best in my profession, and they were in the NBA. My old friend from the Houston Jewish Community Center, Marvin Blumenthal, who had been such good company during all the hours I spent there, was advising me, making sure my enthusiasm for the NBA and San Diego didn't cost me a good deal.

I signed with the Rockets after hearing what Mr. Breitbard had to offer, a salary in six figures, a four-year contract with a clause in it protecting me against being cut or traded without my permission. I knew what I wanted, and Mr. Breitbard did, too, and he gave it to me. He was a fair person offering a fair deal. I wasn't out to stick a gun in his back, so I signed. But I might have cost myself another hundred thousand or two because I loved San Diego so much I might have signed for almost anything just for the pleasure of being able to live and play in San Diego. It was love at first sight when I landed there, when we stayed at the Vacation Village Motel and I said to myself, "This is it. Just let me stay right here forever."

It wasn't meant to stay that way, as so often happens in life, but for that moment, I didn't see how anything could possibly spoil my little slice of Heaven.

Tied up in my decision as to what to do about turning pro was another decision, whether to play for the U.S. team in the '68 Olympics that year. If I did, I wouldn't be able to turn pro until after they were over. If I got hurt, my pro career might be endangered. I felt

I owed America something because it had made all these good things possible, but I felt I also owed something to my family and to myself. My solution was to stipulate in my contract with the Rockets that I would contribute a certain sum to the U.S. Olympic Committee to help pay the team's expenses. I felt that was the best way I could contribute and still be doing the right thing for everyone concerned. Besides, I wasn't even sure I'd make the Olympic team. When I say that, people accuse me of false modesty. But the fact is that I happen to be one of those guys who are poor practice players. I often look awful in practice, but I usually manage to do all right in games. Some players are like that. I know I'm one of them. Even though I was the college Player of the Year and had been the first player picked in both the NBA and the ABA drafts, it's entirely possible I might not have made the Olympic team. In fact, the year before, I tried out for the U.S. team to compete in the Pan-American games. I was a two-time All-American and a highly publicized player, but I got cut. It was those lousy performances in practice.

I also remembered the experience of Bill Russell. A lot of people don't know how he came to play for the Boston Celtics. He played in the Olympics after his great collegiate career at San Francisco. He hurt his knee and had to have an operation. St. Louis had the draft rights to him but when that happened St. Louis traded the rights to Boston for Easy Ed Macauley. St. Louis won the championship one year with Macauley, but then Boston won eleven championships in 13 years with Russell.

There's another problem with playing on U.S. Olympic teams. The other nations of the world subsidize their athletes and, in some cases, they even pay them salaries. A lot of those Olympic athletes our men and women are competing against are as professional as

I am in the NBA. They don't have to worry about paying their own expenses for training or about living expenses for their families and their bills back home. The government takes care of all that.

I don't see how the U.S. teams can ever again be as successful in the Olympics as they once were, and it's because of this. More and more athletes are becoming afraid to jeopardize their prospective professional careers for the honor of representing our nation in the Olympics, and you can't really blame them. And more and more sports are opening up into professional competition, such as tennis and track in recent years. I think the U.S. will continue to lose athletes to the professional ranks, in growing numbers, until we provide for our athletes the way the nations we're competing against do.

When I reported to the Rockets' rookie camp, I knew I was a genius. I had the worst rookie camp in the history of the NBA, and only a genius would have thought to put that clause in my contract guaranteeing that they wouldn't cut me. But once the season started, things were different. The Rockets had won only 15 games the year before, their first season as an expansion club, and lost 67. In my first year with them, we made the playoffs. Everything was right. I led the NBA in scoring, the only rookie except for Wilt Chamberlain to do it, and nobody has done it since. I was second in the league in rebounds. One night in Detroit, after only one month as a pro, I scored 54 points. The headlines were telling the story:

ELVIN'S PRO DEBUT PERKS UP ROCKETS

HAYES' DEFENSE VITAL TO ROCKETS

BIG E'S SHOOTING ORBITS ROCKETS

HAYES CONTINUES TO AMAZE IN EVERY PHASE

BIG E TAKES OVER NBA SCORING LEAD

One writer, after my first year, wrote these words about me:

> "Almost from the moment Elvin donned the Rockets suit, basketball was a success in a clime that features golf courses, tennis courts and white sandy beaches. Suddenly the seashores were barren, the fairways intermittently populated and soft-shoe racquet-wielders were going inside, but not for tennis.
>
> "Hayes, a super scorer, shot-blocker and rebounder, was instantly magnetic...Hayes stays healthy; he keeps pouring in the points, and the fans keep coming out."

That's the way it was that first year for me. We were living a fairy tale. Everything we touched turned to gold, the team staged an incredible comeback and many people gave me a lot of the credit. Fans were pouring out, Mr. Breitbard was happy and nothing could go wrong. I mention those headlines not to brag but to give you an idea of how beautiful everything was that first year, and so you can realize the full impact of how completely things turned on us in our second year. I also quote those headlines because I suspect you'll find it hard to believe, as I did in my second year, that the stories in the second season were being written by the same people and about the same person—me.

In a way, we were the victims of the success we had achieved in my first year. Suddenly some of the players were telling the Rockets' management, "Hey, we made the playoffs, so I want more money."

Don Kojis, who was now thirty years old with six years in the league, laid it right out for all of us players one day at a team meeting when he said, "I'm telling you guys now. I want out of here. No matter what it takes,

I'm getting out." He was unhappy with his contract, and he was making it clear to all of us.

Unfortunately, someone in that meeting also made it clear to the press. The papers got hold of the story and started to write that the glow from the previous year was wearing off with the Rockets, that many of the players—even including Jack McMahon, our coach—had always resented the personal involvement of the owner the year before in signing me to my contract. Now the people were reading that many of the players felt I was making too much money—the papers had reported that I signed for $440,000—and they wanted some of that Breitbard money. Some of those guys were left over from that 15–67 team of only the season before last, but they were suffering from short memories. They were forgetting that they were responsible for that record, and that many people were saying I was responsible for the record that followed, the one that got us into the playoffs my first year on the team.

The team's performance at the start of my second year didn't help matters. We lost our first nine games before finally beating the Warriors on a shot at the buzzer. McMahon was fired. We were losing, and when you lose long enough, the coach gets fired. That's the way it is, and McMahon knew it when he took the job. Casey Stengel used to say the same thing when he was managing the Yankees and the Mets. He said, "The only thing a manager can be sure of is that someday he's going to get fired." That's what happened to McMahon.

Only that's not the way it was reported. McMahon was going around telling the papers that Elvin Hayes had him fired. The same coach who had been giving me so much credit the year before was now giving me all the blame. I was still doing everything I could—scoring, rebounding, playing the best defense I knew how—but McMahon was saying I got him fired.

71

When that happened and the newspaper stories started to appear, I remembered a story Wilt Chamberlain had told me. He said, "They always say Wilt Chamberlain fired the coach, but nobody ever says I hired any." Now I was in the same position as Wilt. I was getting blamed for firing the coach, but I knew from what Wilt told me that nobody would credit me with hiring his replacement.

Jack McMahon had always resented Bob Breitbard's fondness for me. He didn't like it when Mr. Breitbard decided to handle the negotiations with me himself. From the beginning, Jack always felt I had the upper hand over him. Nothing could be further from the truth. I never even talked to the owner about the coach or his performance. I was a rookie trying to make it in a league where others had failed. I needed all the concentration and effort I could muster, and I couldn't afford any distractions or disagreements or running feuds with anyone, especially my boss, the coach. That was true in my rookie year, and it was true again in my second year, when the trouble started and McMahon was fired. One good season didn't guarantee me permanent success in the NBA and I knew it. I wanted my second year to prove my rookie season was no fluke, that I really was that good, so again I didn't want any distractions or arguments or feuds.

The coach was fired because we were losing. It was that simple. It usually is in sports. And when that happens and there is a big-name player on the team, it will sometimes follow that the coach says the star got him fired. And sometimes I'm sure it really is that way. But it wasn't this time.

So McMahon was gone and I was getting the blame not only for his firing but for the team's bad season. We still weren't playing well, we were losing and now the writers were saying Elvin Hayes is a troublemaker, a malcontent. I was still doing everything I knew how to do—scoring, rebounding, playing aggressive defense and ranking among the league leaders in every department—and yet I was reading in the papers that the team was losing because of me. The same writers who had been writing all the great stories about me under those happy headlines the year before were watching me do the same things the next season, only now all of a sudden I'm making the team into a loser.

I had never had trouble with writers before. I played under the very close eye of writers at the University of Houston for four years and never had any trouble with them. And I never had any trouble with the writers when I was playing in Houston again with the Rockets after the team moved there from San Diego before the 1971–72 season. Even with the same team and the same players, the writers covering us were no problem—but they were different writers.

One San Diego writer, Tom Callahan, developed a particular dislike for me. It was almost as if he were a homing pigeon who had homed in on me and was determined to get me. He was always friendly enough in person, smiling and showing no problems on the surface. Then his paper comes out with a story by him zinging me for first one thing and then another.

Finally, at a game one night, I told him, "Hey, man, why don't you just get away from me and stay away?" The next day, there's another article rapping me.

One of the reasons I was able to bear up under all this was that the fans, the good people of San Diego, never gave up on me. They never booed me, never quit on me. My mail was just as nice as ever, even nicer with all the letters I received supporting me in my hour of trial. The experience could have destroyed me, or any other kid of 24. I owe so much to those fine people.

They probably don't know to this day that they helped a young man survive—and that's the right word—survive a terrible period of torment and anxiety and real suffering.

That's how bad that time was. I was discouraged, confused, physically sick, and I had always been the healthiest guy in the world. But here I was, suddenly a famous star after only one season in the NBA, a shining hero to the people of my city, getting lavish praise every day in the press and then, just as suddenly, I'm the target of nasty newspaper articles, mean charges from my coach, ugly comments from some of my teammates.

I didn't know what to do. I had no place to hide. Criticism in the press was something new to me, and so was playing on a team with dissension. I was up against a completely strange and bewildering experience, and there was no way I could have prepared for it beforehand or solved it myself when it struck. There are no courses you can take in college to teach you how to handle that kind of a problem. Books can't really help you. You have to experience it, to live through it, to learn how to cope with it. That's a painful, depressing and almost panicky experience if you're only 24 years old, you're away from home and all the pressure in the world is on you, and now you're reading a lot of mean and nasty things about yourself. All you can do is try to hang on and hope you can make it through all your troubles, but you're not sure you can.

When the Rockets fired McMahon they hired Alex Hannum. Alex had the makings of a fine professional coach. He had one of the best offensive minds in the NBA. He could have helped us tremendously as a team and he could have helped the young players individually, including me. Instead, he does things like singling out Rudy Tomjanovich and saying he'd never make it in the NBA. Today Rudy is one of the NBA's stars, but in San Diego he never got off the bench.

Alex came into the Rockets' job having been told I was uncoachable and a troublemaker. All through college and in my rookie year with the Rockets people said I was highly coachable and no trouble at all. Now all of a sudden supposedly I'm different. So Hannum comes into the job convinced by others that he has to break me. I was as vulnerable as a buck private at the mercy of a drill sergeant.

Hannum started on me right away. I'm a very sensitive person. I admit it. I'm not ashamed of it. I make no apologies for it. I don't like being hollered at and cursed at. I didn't like it at San Diego or any other place before or since.

If it's wrong to be a sensitive human being, then that's just the way it will have to be. I don't think any human being likes to be hollered at, and I don't mind admitting it in my own case. You can beat me or whip me or kick me and I can get over it. But to holler at me and yell unkind things at me and curse me—these things cut into me deeply. I can forgive you for that, because God tells us to forgive, but I can't forget it. That kind of thing stays with me and keeps on hurting.

Hannum jumped me for anything at all. He was on me constantly. It was Hayes this and Hayes that. Hayes-Hayes-Hayes!

Alex left town one afternoon and flew to Denver. He negotiated a deal which made him president, general manager and coach of the Nuggets. He flew back to San Diego and said he was quitting. He did it all on his own and he came up with what sounded to everyone like a fantastic deal for himself.

So then the papers reported that Elvin Hayes got Alex Hannum fired. As long as they were wrong, how come they didn't also give me credit for lining up that great deal for him? Alex Hannum wasn't fired at all. He went out and got a better job for himself and then came back and told the Rockets' front office about it. They were as surprised as anyone else.

I didn't know who our new coach would be, but I knew one thing: I was glad people wouldn't be coming up to me the way they had been and say, "I was talking to Alex the other day. You know, he really doesn't like you."

Hannum's successor was Tex Winters. I was wondering if I could ever be happy again. The team was moved from San Diego to Houston, but even that return to my scene of glory and happiness didn't help. As much as I loved San Diego, I said I'd be glad to get back to Houston. That also managed to get reported in a way that gave some people the wrong idea, and if they were misled by the stories quoting me on that statement, I apologize. What I was really saying was that leaving San Diego would enable me to escape the tensions and the pressures caused by some of our players and aggravated by the press. But the move didn't solve the problem, it merely moved it.

In Houston we still had some chronic complainers on the team and coaches who couldn't handle it, so they took the easy way out—zing the big name. The press was better, but the atmosphere within the organization wasn't. And I was still the fall guy, still the one taking all the blame for the team's troubles.

There didn't seem to be any relief from the burden or any clearing away of the confusion. I couldn't understand why my world had turned sour so suddenly and dramatically. I escaped from adults and spent as much time as I could with kids, something I had always done and still do. The people who know me will tell you that, and I never have done it for publicity. I do it because I love kids. The kids were loyal to me too, just like all the fans in San Diego and all the wonderful people of Houston. In San Diego, it was the writers and some players and coaches who were causing me such deep agony. In Houston, the writers were better, but the bitter fighting and gossip within the organization was no better at all.

In San Diego, I would take long walks by myself on the sandy white beaches, the same way I would escape to that bayou across the street from the U of H while I was in college. I would try to sort out the pieces, see what I had done wrong and hope that out of those answers would come a solution to my problems. But I could find no answers. I knew things were not my fault, so it was not within my power to change or to correct them. The change had to come from the source of the problems, and that wasn't happening.

Erna used to watch me in my torment and ask me, "Why don't you pray?"

I used to answer, "Prayer is for those who need it, and I don't need it."

I was wrong, and I can see that now, but God had not yet come into my life in any way that meant anything to me, and I was not going to turn to God only because I needed help. I would turn to God later, for positive reasons, not because I was desperate.

One day I was running on the beach, staying in shape and maybe trying to run from my problems as well, when I came across a little boy eight years old. We started talking. He was a cute little kid and he attracted my attention quickly. I asked him where he was from.

"Washington State."

"Where are you staying."

He pointed to his family's car. "Over there."

He, his mother, a friend, two sisters and a brother were all staying together—in that car. The oldest child was only about twelve.

I found out more about the family. It turned out that his mother (there was no father) had lost her job in Washington and couldn't find another, so she packed everyone into her old car and they headed for Southern California, where she hoped for better luck.

I took them to a motel in Mission Beach and paid a week's rent in advance and told them to relax and start enjoying their stay. Then I went to a friend of mine who owned a restaurant and got the mother a job as a cook. Then I moved them after that week into an apartment and paid the rent for the first two months.

I never bothered to tell them who I was, and I'm not sure they've ever found out. I never saw them again. I didn't have to. I knew they were on their feet and things would be all right now. And I didn't want any publicity because I wasn't doing it for publicity. I was doing it because people needed help and I was able to provide it. I was thankful just to be able to do it.

But nobody could help me. The torture within me continued. The thought of suicide even entered my mind, but I dismissed it quickly. That never solved any problem. In this case, it would only have removed my problem from me but it would have given other problems to other people like Erna and little Elvin and my mother and others. That was no answer.

I was taking sleeping pills, a guy who never had a bit of trouble sleeping and still doesn't. I was taking stomach pills, and I never had stomach problems before and haven't since. I was calling the doctor at four in the morning. My nerves were shattered, and people tell me I'm the calmest guy they know.

I'm sure all of this would have come as a shock to the fans, the writers, my teammates and everyone else. People just assumed that I was on top of the world. After all, I was a big sports star, wasn't I? I was making all kinds of money, wasn't I? What problems can a guy like that possibly have?

But you never know. Believe me, you never know. I've tried to learn from those awful times, just as I try to learn from my every experience in life—but in the past few years, after I found so much happiness with the Bullets and the fine people of Washington, I tried to put those terrible years out of my mind. They came back to me, though, when Freddie Prinze, the co-star of "Chico and the Man," shot himself to death. He was almost the same age I was when I was having my problems, 22. Then a couple of Washington writers stirred things up again.

I can understand some of the pressures Freddie Prinze must have felt. They may have been different kinds, but I can understand the torment he must have been going through at the same age, trying to cope with so many demands on him to perform at a level of excellence every day in his profession, trying to handle the heavy load of a career that gave him so much fame and fortune and then, as hard as that is at such a young age, having other problems thrust on him that he felt powerless to cope with. I can identify with that.

I have always been blessed with a wonderful family, and if it hadn't been for them I might never have pulled through my own crisis. But Freddie was spared one problem that was a major cause of my difficulties— the writers.

As harsh and untrue as some of their stories were, I'm sure they didn't really mean to put me through the torture I was enduring, and I'm sure they would have been stunned, probably even apologetic, if they had ever been able to know what I was going through. But writers should stop and think sometimes before they sit down at their typewriters. They should consider the possible effect of what they are about to write if they're criticizing someone. Their words can have a powerful effect on the athlete or the politician or the entertainer, and many times the effect can spread to other lives as well, to family, friends, business associates.

Just to write or say something which seems harmless enough—that the writer thinks so-and-so has lost a step, or so-and-so's fastball seems to have lost just a little bit of its fire, or this guy has bad hands in the writer's opinion or that guy has trouble defending against the pass in the announcer's opinion—can have a tremendous effect, maybe permanent, on an athlete's career. If it's not true, and turns out to be an inaccurate statement, that may not help. The truth never catches up with the lie. And the effect on his life may be just as harmful as the effect on his career, maybe worse.

And if a writer is about to do a story on a person's character and temperament, he has within his typewriter the ability to brand that athlete the same way some writers branded me. I like to think those writers never really intended to do me the harm they did, but that was the result. It's a result which lingers even today. I think I've managed to live down my reputation of my early years in the NBA, but every once in a while something will crop up to show me that some people still remember, and a few—fortunately only a very few—still believe that maybe there was something to those stories. It was this lingering reputation which contributed to trouble with some Washington writers after we lost to Houston in the 1977 playoffs.

I'm thankful, though, the fans never deserted me. I've played pro ball in four cities—San Diego, Houston, Baltimore and Washington—and the fans are still just as loyal and just as nice and just as respectful toward me as they ever were.

Thanks to them and to Erna, her family and my mother and my family, I survived my ordeal. Through it all, I never really changed. I've been with the Bullets five seasons now and I've never had a minute's trouble with the organization or the fans, even though the writers and I disagree from time to time. I hope I stay with the Bullets and Pollin, our owner, and the great people of the Washington area forever. That's my wish.

Prayers saved me, prayers from other people. After telling Erna I didn't need prayers, I'd sneak away and say, "God, please help me." But I wasn't really praying. I wasn't really glorifying God. I was just pleading to save my own neck.

I am convinced that prayers saved me, but I think the credit goes to the prayers of others, not to those SOS signals I was sending up to Heaven. I thank God that He never let my awful trial destroy me, that He instead gave me the strength to keep on functioning as a basketball player and as a person.

At that time I had no way of knowing that He had other plans for me, but He knew it. Today I say prayers of thanksgiving to God, every day, for coming into my life later.

6

CHANGING A ROCKET INTO A BULLET

My deliverance proves that the Lord really does work in strange and wondrous ways. The Rockets were playing a game in Seattle at the same time that the NBA owners were meeting there. One day I happened to run into the owner of the Bullets, Abe Pollin, and his wife in the hotel lobby. I was telling them how much I'd love to play for the Bullets.

"I can't talk to him," I said to Mrs. Pollin, "but I can talk to you." Mr. Pollin and I both had to be careful so we would not put him in a position where he could be accused of "tampering" with a player under contract to another club. After a little more conversation, we went our separate ways.

Tex Winters was trying to convert me into a different kind of basketball player. After he succeeded Alex Hannum, he called me aside and said, "I want you to become a passer." It was like telling a home-run hitter to stop hitting homers and start bunting instead.

I've always been a scorer. That's what I do best, although I'm always among the league leaders in other departments, too—rebounding, blocked shots, minutes played. But scoring is what I do best, it's what I'm most valuable to my team for and it's one of the things I get paid for.

But the coach told me to do it, so I tried. But now, for the first time in my life, I was getting my shots blocked because I was looking for an opportunity to pass first, then taking the shot only when nobody was open for a pass. I was giving away my quickness because my man was able to catch up with me while I was looking for a passing opportunity. My size isn't the main reason for my scoring. It's always been my quickness. I can beat most men with it. Now I was giving up that quickness, and my opponents were getting a hand in my face when they couldn't before.

One day I told my roommate, Stu Lantz, "I've

84

given this experiment enough time. From now on, I'm going to shoot."

I came out shooting that night and I scored something like 37 points and racked up 20 or more rebounds. I was my old self again, I was helping the team far more than I had been during the experiment by Tex Winters, and everything seemed right again.

Winters pulled me aside and said, "You're fighting me."

I would have found that kind of a reaction hard to believe, but after the three coaches I had played for in the NBA, I could believe any kind of reaction imaginable on the part of a coach. So I kept my patience and my manners and tried to explain things to him in a respectful way.

"Look, Coach," I said, "I tried to do it but I can't because I lose my quickness and then I can't help the team. I'll keep on playing my hardest for you and do my best for you but I can help you most of all by scoring."

He still thought I was fighting him.

"Coach," I went on, "I feel I can help you more with my scoring ability than I can as a passing center."

He said I was too short, that he needed a 7-footer. So before the next season started, he acquired Otto Moore, who is only an inch under 7 feet. The Rockets still didn't win, and Winters was fired.

At the end of the season, before Winters got Moore for the Rockets, I told their front office, "Look, if you guys want me to take all the blame for this team, if you want me to bear all the burden and carry all the frustrations for the whole team, you're going to have to pay me more money."

I wasn't really looking for money, but I wasn't going to carry the whole load without getting something more for it. By now I had entered into an arrangement with Al Ross from the First United Management Corporation of Los Angeles. Al and I met with officials of the team and told them either they stopped pointing at me every time somebody did something wrong or they paid me more money for shouldering everyone's mistakes or they traded me. Any of the three was fine with me.

Their answer was that they probably would agree to a raise, but one of the owners was out of the country. They thought he would agree, but they wanted to talk to him when he returned. They'd be in touch. Al and I said fine. We also told them I had four choices in case of a trade—the New York Knicks, the Los Angeles Lakers, the Boston Celtics and the Baltimore Bullets. I also said I hoped we could avoid a trade and straighten the problem out. Lord knows I love Houston, I still live there and I didn't want to leave. But something had to give. I couldn't go on the way things were, and I'm not sure how many people could have put up with them as long as I had.

I was working that summer as special-events co-ordinator for the city's summer recreation program. Less than a week later, I was in my car driving to another recreation event when I heard on the car radio that I had been traded. The Rockets had sent me to the Bullets. In return, they were getting Jack Marin. To this day I tell people it was the trade Mrs. Pollin made.

Things still were happening in a weird pattern. A contract problem developed as a result of the trade. It was discovered that my original contract with the Rockets violated California law because it was for one year more than allowed under the state's labor laws. Because it had been signed in the state—in San Diego—there was some question as to whether it was a valid contract. So now I needed to know: Am I a free agent or not?

The usual sparring around between player and club followed, and we were headed to court. The Texas law firm of Leon Jaworski, who later became the Special

86

Watergate Prosecutor, was representing me. Thirty minutes before the case was to begin, Abe Pollin asked if he and I could go off into a room by ourselves. I said sure.

So we left our lawyers to talk to themselves, while Mr. Pollin and I closed the door and started talking, just the two of us, one-on-one. We came to an agreement with no problem, and I found Mr. Pollin, as I had Mr. Breitbard in San Diego, to be one of the finest men anyone could ever work for. I like him and respect him a great deal. And Mrs. Pollin is just as great. I just pray hard that God will grant my request to let Abe Pollin win a championship before I retire. That's my one remaining ambition in basketball—to win an NBA championship for Mr. Pollin and his wife, as well as for myself.

A feeling like that toward my owner is important to me. Even though I'm called a star and I get paid a high salary, money really isn't everything to me. I know people say that about themselves, but in my case it really isn't. Respect and friendship and an attitude of mutual trust are more important. I feel all those things toward Abe.

Not many athletes and owners feel that way toward each other anymore, and maybe it's more the fault of the athletes than the owners. I'm well-paid, but I'm far from being the highest-paid professional athlete, or even the highest-paid basketball player—and yet, nobody should be making as much money as I am for playing a game.

Schoolteachers and ministers and police officers all have trouble making ends meet, while people in pro sports and entertainment draw salaries which fans have trouble believing. It seems to feed on itself, too. Free agents and first-round draft choices make demands that the fans, who are paying our salaries, can't even comprehend, much less agree with. And as the situation continues and worsens, our sense of values gets twisted all out of reality and morality—and that's the biggest danger of all.

Here's Julius Erving, making a lot of money with the New York Nets. The ABA and the NBA merge and—boom!—he wants to renegotiate his contract or be traded or declared a free agent or Lord knows what else.

Someone asked him whether he should have felt some loyalty to his old team, which had been paying him so well and had given the opportunity to become the biggest star in the ABA. According to the papers, Julius answered by saying, "Loyalty doesn't enter into it. That is a term of another era. Today the market value of a player is dictated by what the people are willing to pay."

Loyalty—a term of another era?

There's got to be a stopping point somewhere. All those business geniuses who own professional sports teams are going to have to put their foot down sooner or later, and probably sooner. Professional sports will either all go broke, or only the multimillionaire club-owners in the very largest cities like New York and Los Angeles will be able to compete.

No athlete is worth the money he's getting, including me, and we ought to be honest enough to admit it.

Not only that, as if the salaries aren't bad enough, it's making for a lot of awfully dull sports stories in the papers. Now all we ever read about anymore is this guy's demands or that guy's demands or strikes by the players' association or the referees or some other dull thing. The fans are getting tired of seeing their sports pages covered with stories about salaries and strikes and court cases.

I consider myself a sports fan, too, not just a

professional athlete, and I think I'm right when I say they're getting tired of reading about some guy demanding $400,000 a year while the fans are making $9,000 and are worrying about whether they'll ever reach $12,000. When they pick up the sports page, they just want to know who won last night's game.

So now I was a Bullet, and that bad dream, which had started out to be such a beautiful one in my first season and turned into a nightmare lasting the next three years, turned beautiful again. The Bullets were a good team. I knew that because we had never been able to beat them. They had Wes Unseld and Earl Monroe and Archie Clark and Kevin Loughery and Gus Johnson. But I was searching for more than just a good team and a good owner. I was praying for a good coach, too, and when I found Gene Shue I knew right away my prayers had been answered.

I was coming to the Bullets with a bad reputation. I knew that and Gene knew it. I've always been totally honest with myself about myself, about my abilities and inabilities, about my strengths and weaknesses and about my sensitivities. I knew I was now saddled with the reputation of a troublemaker, a malcontent, a guy who causes trouble on every team he plays for. It was the exact opposite of my reputation over nine years of high school, college and my first season in San Diego. It was unjust and untrue, but it was there and I knew it.

The simple fact that the Bullets were willing to take me told me something. It told me that either they thought or knew I wasn't that way or they were at least willing to take a chance that I would find happiness and harmony, again, with them. They were right on both points.

Not long after the trade, I met with Coach Shue. He laid it right out there for me. "All the stuff you got in

San Diego and Houston is over," he said. I could barely stay in my chair. I felt like jumping through the ceiling and shouting, "Hallelujah!"

"When you come here," Gene told me, "nobody is going to blame you if we lose. Nobody is going to say anything if you miss a shot or commit a turnover. Just play ball, Elvin. Forget all that other junk. It's all over."

Getting the chance to play for Abe Pollin and Gene Shue was one of the greatest things that has ever happened to me. Gene made me a complete basketball player. He said other players could and would help out, that I didn't have to worry anymore about doing everything myself. I have always felt, and still do, that my job is to play every phase of the game and that my team, whoever that team is, depends on me, in that sense, to do everything—to score, play tough defense, rebound, block shots, set picks and, yes, even pass, although some people refuse to believe the last one. Some writers have misunderstood that frank belief on my part, that I have to do everything. I don't say others shouldn't be doing some or all of those things, too, but I *do* say that any team I'm playing for is depending on me to carry the lion's share of the load in all those departments. And when I say this, that doesn't mean I'm complaining. I'm merely stating the role my team depends on me to fulfill, like Johnny Bench saying his team depends on him to be a great catcher and hit a lot of home runs and drive in a lot of runs. Nobody would get upset if Bench said that, and he's probably said it a hundred times. So why get upset when I say my team depends on me?

Coach Shue worked especially hard with me on my passing and my shot selection. I owe an awful lot to him, and I'll always be grateful for everything he did with me and for me. I hope he wins a championship someday. He's just been fired as the coach of the 76ers, but he's a fine coach and deserves to win it all.

When Gene left the Bullets, a funny thing happened, or didn't happen. No writer in Baltimore or Washington said Elvin Hayes had the coach fired. I thought then that my deliverance was complete.

After Gene I found myself playing under my fifth pro coach in only five seasons, K.C. Jones, the former Boston Celtics great. Kase was another tremendous coach and tremendous person. I became very close to him and his family. K.C. picked up with me where Gene left off, and I was able to continue to improve my individual skills and my value to my team.

When he left, it was because management fired him, not me. We had exploded through the season with the incredible record of 60 wins and 22 losses and won our way to the NBA finals, only to lose in four straight to Golden State in one of the biggest upsets in pro basketball history. The following season we dropped off badly and barely made it into the playoffs, then lost to Cleveland in the first round. The Bullets thought a change of coaches was necessary, and the papers were reporting that I was so upset about his firing that I might ask to be traded. They were right. That's how loyal I was to both of my coaches with the Bullets, Gene Shue and K.C.

My Bullets' coaches have helped me so much, including our present boss, Dick Motta. Our general manager, Bob Ferry, was good enough to help get me from the Rockets, and he was effective enough to have nothing but good coaches handling us. Dick Motta uses an offense which is designed to get the ball to his forwards down low and he likes to run. Both features are my kind of basketball. Motta also believes in using his bench, and he does it effectively.

God and my Bullets' coaches have helped me get

control of my life. They have put the joy back in basketball for me. I don't feel tormented anymore, even when
the writers criticize me.

Correction
In a question-and-answer interview with Elvin
Hayes in Wednesday's sports section, the word
"hell" was incorrectly attributed as part of one of
Hayes' answers.
Hayes actually said "well."
The *Post* regrets the error.

That item appeared in the Washington Post *on April
14, 1977. If you don't know Elvin Hayes, it tells you a little
something about him. If you do know him, the item
doesn't surprise you at all. On the contrary, any friend of
Elvin Hayes reading the* Washington Post *of the day
before had to be either stunned or skeptical, stunned that
Elvin said "hell" or skeptical that he really said it.*

*People have known The Big E for years
without hearing him say "damn" or "hell," except when
talking about sin and damnation. He regards them as curse
words, "and I don't curse." He doesn't complain when
others do, nor does he try to get them to change their
vocabulary to suit his, where the most violent word is
"shucks." The language others use is their business, but he
won't change his just to match theirs.*

*His language, like his plain way of life, is a
reflection of his Christian beliefs. He doesn't wear his beliefs
on his sleeve. He doesn't go around soapbox in hand
preaching on every corner yelling to the world to wake up
before it's too late. Like everything else about him,
Elvin Hayes' Christianity is calm.*

It is there, however, no less real, no less deep than

the Christianity of others, yet tested more than that of others in a profession which every day beckons with temptations which the rest of us are never called on to endure.

Forty-one games out of town—all those nights in hotels in other cities, all those chances to go astray in any number of different ways. But Elvin Hayes is seldom seen on the road trips. While his teammates may be out on the town at night, Elvin can be found in his room, by himself, watching an old movie or a ballgame, maybe remembering when Savannah Hayes couldn't afford a TV set for her kids. During the day, it's either a little sightseeing, usually by himself, or more time alone in his room, reading the Bible. He'll see his teammates at mealtime, but seldom at any other time.

It's not unusual for Elvin Hayes to give a speech at a church while the Bullets are on the road. It may turn out to be good preparation. He's thinking about becoming a minister when his basketball days are over. If not as an ordained minister, it is clear to all who know him that Elvin Hayes will continue to practice his Christian beliefs, not just on Sundays at the Bible Way Pentecostal Church in Houston but seven days a week. He'll do it every way he can, not in a preachy way, not in pounding on a pulpit in hellfire-and-brimstone oratory but in living life the way Elvin Hayes thinks God wants him to, and in helping anyone he can find who needs help.

It wasn't always this way with Elvin Hayes. He remembers how it was before, and how he thought about God and searched for Him and tried for so long to tie it all together in a way Elvin could understand. And he remembers how it finally happened that his search ended and he found God.

For a long time I wondered about a relationship with

93

God, why it was so difficult for me to establish one. I had been taught about God when I was a boy and I went to church and Sunday school every week with my mother and my brothers and sisters. But that's not finding God. It's fine as far as it goes, but it doesn't go far enough, not for me.

I have felt the need for a real relationship with God during most of my adult years. Even those times of trial and torment with the Rockets in San Diego and again in Houston did not produce the relationship I was seeking, even though they did drive me to ask for God's help.

That wasn't the fulfillment I had been seeking. It was just a case of screaming for help. When the help came in the form of my trade to the Bullets, the satisfaction of knowing God still did not come. It just meant that everyone's prayers had been answered. The relationship I was looking for still wasn't there.

I remember when the relationship started to form for me. It was after my first season with the Bullets. I was back home in Houston with my family in the summer of 1973. It was Sunday morning. Erna and I used to go to different churches, and I had already gone that morning. I was cutting the lawn while Erna prepared to go to her service at the Bible Way Pentecostal Church.

Suddenly I got the idea to go with her. I enjoyed the church I had been attending, but the relationship with God still had not come. I put the lawnmower away and walked back inside and told Erna I'd like to go with her.

During the service, the minister, the Reverend Elba Parker, said, "Elvin Hayes, come here." He was standing in front of the congregation and pointing toward Erna and me. It was my first time there, so I thought he meant Erna.

Elvin Hayes beats Bill Walton of Portland to the basket for a slam-dunk.
Photo by Jerry Wachter Photography Ltd.

Playing with a broken nose, Elvin Hayes beats Kareem Abdul-Jabbar to a rebound. In a nine-year pro career, Hayes has missed only four games out of 800.
Photo by Richard Darcey Washington Post

The Big E fakes out Kareem Abdul-Jabbar and leaves him
waving to score against the Lakers.
Photo by Richard Darcey, Washington Post

The glory of a slam-dunk.
Photo by Richard Darcey, Washington Post
◄

The Big E goes high to score despite the leaping Darnell Hillman of Indiana. *Photo by Richard Darcey, Washington Post*

Houston's Elvin Hayes and UCLA's Lew Alcindor (now Kareem Abdul-Jabbar) go up for the opening jump in the NCAA playoffs in Louisville in 1967. The Bruins won, but the stage was set for the biggest game in college basketball history one year later. ▶

This was the scene when the University of Houston defeated UCLA, 71–69, before 52,693 fans and 50 million TV viewers in what many still consider college basketball's greatest game ever. The loss snapped UCLA's 47-game winning streak and, in a matchup of superstars, Elvin Hayes outscored Kareem Abdul-Jabbar, 39–15, outrebounded him, 15–12, scored his team's first 6 points and scored the winning 2 points on a pair of free throws with 34 seconds left. The setting is Houston's Astrodome. The date, January 20, 1968.

Two members of
Washington's Catholic Youth
Organization present Elvin Hayes
a special award for being voted
the most popular player
on the Bullets.

Elvin Hayes, a superstar who gives more time to community causes than almost any other professional athlete in any sport, helps 5-year-old Robert to learn how to use his legs while worker Ita Killeen guides their efforts. The Big E has spent a great deal of time working for kids like Robert through the District of Columbia Society for Crippled Children. *U.S. News Service Photo*

It's no way to treat a former teammate, but Elvin Hayes blocks Detroit's Kevin Porter with a thigh to the body, helping Larry Wright to get open for a shot. *Photo by Richard Darcey, Washington Post*

Elvin Hayes reaches
the rim to score against
Boston. *Photo by
Jerry Wachter,
Photography Ltd.*

The Big E is on the floor fighting for a loose ball against Buffalo. *Photo by Jerry Wachter, Photography Ltd.*

Elvin Hayes grabs another of his more than 10,000 rebounds. He was only the twelfth player in the history of the NBA to reach that figure, achieving it four months before teammate Wes Unseld. *Photo by Jerry Wachter, Photography Ltd.*
▶

Elvin Hayes lets out a scream of elation as he slams home another dunk shot in front of teammate Mitch Kupchak. *Photo by Gary N. Fine*

The Big E goes high to put up a shot against Atlanta. *Photo by Gary N. Fine*

Controversial but always consulted, Elvin Hayes takes time to talk to reporters in front of his locker after a post-game shower. *Photo by Gary N. Fine*

The flawless form of Elvin Hayes scoring on a jump shot in front of Garfield Heard. *Photo by Jerry Wachter, Photography Ltd.*

▶

Elvin Hayes meets President and Mrs. Ford at the White House during a prayer brunch for athletes at the White House. Hayes delivered the invocation, a prayer written by his wife, Erna, and himself.
AP Wirephoto

Elvin Hayes goes to work on Houston's Moses Malone.
Photo by Gary N. Fine
◄

Bullets' owner Abe Pollin, a 6-footer himself, enjoys a dressing-room visit with his superstar. The Big E says his last ambition in basketball is "to win an NBA championship for Abe Pollin."
Photo by Gary N. Fine
►

Two giants of professional basketball fight it out in front of the basket— The Big E and Dr. J, Julius Erving of the Philadelphia 76ers.
Photo by Richard Darcey
Washington Post

Elvin Hayes drives hard to score against Don Chaney of the Celtics, his teammate at the University of Houston and still his good friend.
Photo by Richard Darcey Washington Post

The concentration of Elvin Hayes at the foul line. He is nearly a 70 percent free-throw shooter.
Photo by Richard Darcey, Washington Post

Elvin Hayes puts on a power move to get inside Boston's John Havlicek for 2 points.
Photo by Richard Darcey Washington Post

Bob McAdoo goes high but not high enough, so Elvin Hayes scores.
Photo by Richard Darcey, Washington Post

One Washington superstar succeeds another. Elvin Hayes follows Larry Brown of the Redskins as Chairman of the American Cancer Society's "IQ" (I Quit Smoking) campaign in the Washington area.
Photo by Jerry Wachter, Photography Ltd.

Elvin Hayes blocks a shot by Atlanta's Joe Meriweather. This unusual view was captured by Photographer Gary Fine from a catwalk high over the playing floor at the Bullets' home, Capital Centre.

"You'd better go up there," I said. "He's talking to you."

Just then the minister spoke again and pointed again: "Elvin Hayes, come here." This time there was no question about it. He was saying Elvin, not Erna.

I stood up and walked forward slowly, not having any idea of what was in store for me. When I reached the front of the church, Reverend Parker told me in front of all those people that Christ loved me and died for me. By itself that message did not end my search. I knew those things already. I still needed something more. I was sure there had to be more to God than Sunday.

Then Reverend Parker suggested I spend some time reading the Bible, concentrating on the Gospel of Matthew. He told me to try those messages for myself. He said Christ had told us, "Enter into a closet and pray secretly to the Father He will answer you in the open."

So I decided to follow that advice, except I didn't go into a closet. But I did go into a room alone and closed the door. I was willing to try this means of finding Him.

As I read and thought, and prayed, things came into focus in my mind. It began to dawn on me that I had been almost a nightmare person after my troubles began in San Diego, and I had not really improved any since my problems had been solved. I began to see that I had turned ugly inside, and now I wasn't very pleased with what I saw in myself. I had no foundation in life. I was too worried about Elvin Hayes.

Over the next few days I continued to read the Bible and sort things out. Suddenly the verses were beginning to make sense, I was realizing and understanding things which I had never even thought of before. I was forming a relationship with God.

All this talk may sound corny or phony, but it's

neither. I don't go around talking about God all day or waving my arms and preaching to the world to repent, but I don't avoid it, or back off when writers or fans ask me about the subject.

Just like all the other subjects people ask athletes about, I've never backed off the subject of religion. Neither have others like Kareem Abdul-Jabbar and George Foreman and George Foster. I feel a person's religious beliefs and church work are as public or as private as they choose to make them. That's why I don't go around shouting about religion and morality. I know I am a born-again Christian. I arrived there in accordance with God's will and His timetable. I prefer not to go around all day preaching at the top of my lungs, but I don't deny my Christian faith, either. I try to live it and practice it while leaving others to their own beliefs and their own ways.

Sometimes God won't let you find peace until you're where He wants you. Looking back, I know now that's why I was having trouble forming a relationship with Him. He wanted me to build a foundation in life, based in turn on a foundation with Him, but I wasn't doing it. After Reverend Parker got me started in the right direction, the relationship came, and so did my peace.

I realize now what I didn't before: I'm not good for anything in life on a permanent basis except for the ministry of God. There are a lot of things in life I'd like to do for myself after I finish playing basketball, but I know I wouldn't be successful at them because He has other things in store for me. My own belief is that no matter what you want to do in life, if it isn't what God wants, He'll put something in your way. By the same token, if it is what God wants, you will succeed no matter what. I honestly believe that.

Nothing else is as important to me in life as that

belief, that with God everything is possible but without Him nothing has value. If I can help save one life, or help save one soul from being destroyed, if I can help make another's life a better life, then I will have done God's will and my life will be fulfilled. That's why I feel you have to have a relationship with God, something between just you and Him, so you can know He is real in your heart, you can feel Him in you. When you have that feeling, as I now have, then you know God can have an effect on your life and you can have an effect on others.

I won't feel any sadness when my time comes to leave basketball. I'll miss my teammates and the fans and the reporters, but that's all. I won't miss the glory, and I won't even miss the money. That's because I will be hearing and spreading a new message: Try God. I may do it as a minister or a church worker or in some other way, but I know I'll do it one way or another because that is God's will.

I'll point out to people that they try other things. They try cigarettes even though they know smoking can kill them. They try whisky even though they know liquor can kill you or even make you kill someone else, like on Saturday nights back in Rayville. So why not try God? What do you have to lose? If you find happiness and a real meaning for your life, then it was certainly worth it. If you don't, what have you lost? And I'll tell people, "Don't take my word for it. Try it yourself." That's my message. It's a simple one, but Christ's own message is simple, too. Mine is part of His.

I spoke at an Episcopalian Church in New Jersey a few years ago during a Bullets' road trip, and I was offering that same message. I told the group that we seem to be building on the wrong things during so much of our lives. We seem to build on things that crumble and fall, but God and His message are forever. Again, I told them we should try God.

After I finished, a man came up to me and said, "I've been looking all my life for what you said today." He was 79 years old.

It's not unusual for me to speak to church groups when we're on the road. I make sure I get plenty of rest and eat the right foods, but I don't mind leaving the hotel long enough to talk to a church audience. I'm a loner on the road anyhow. We each have a private room—with a king-size bed in each—and we get $25 a day to eat on, which is barely enough when you're 6-9 or 7 feet tall. I take my Bible on the road and read it almost constantly. It gives me confidence. It's beginning to look a little frayed and it really isn't that old, but I like worn-looking Bibles. It shows they're being used.

Some people criticize me for being a loner on the road and not long ago the *Washington Post* ran a story saying my loner ways were a problem and suggesting those ways were one of the reasons we weren't playing well at the time. I was interviewed about it on TV at halftime the next night and so were the two writers who cover us. It was a big deal, for one day.

I don't ask anyone to be around me, and I don't ask to be around anyone. I don't try to force the players to like me or dislike me. Some of my teammates and some of the press and some of the public might doubt my beliefs and make fun of them and think I'm some kind of weirdo or religious freak. I can't worry about that or waste my time even thinking about it. I am the way I am and others are the way they are, and that's just the way it is. We ought to be mature enough and Christian enough to accept that and respect each other and get along in harmony. As St. Paul said, "By the grace of God, I am what I am."

A lot of people call me religious, but I'm not sure

that's the right term. There are many different religions. I think I would prefer to be thought of as a Christian, one who is following Christ and trying to obey His word.

I have friends, good friends, who don't share my beliefs. They don't read the Bible or go to church or pray. They don't even believe in God. That's their privilege. They're still my friends. I still love my friends and respect them, and they feel the same about me, but I don't try to change them and they don't try to change me.

My religion and my beliefs are no problem with my teammates or other players in the NBA. They don't let something like that change relationships, but they can't resist the chance to kid me.

Sometimes I'll be bumping my man around on defense and he'll say, "Hey, man, you're supposed to be religious. You shouldn't be knocking me around like this."

Or I'll be taking more of a pounding than should be allowed and I'll call out to the official, "Get him off my back!"

And my opponent will answer before the ref and say, "Careful, E. You're religious. You're not supposed to complain."

Otto Moore, Phil Jackson and Kevin Porter give me more needling than anyone else in the league. They're always on me, and I enjoy it as much as they do. I'm as serious as anyone could be about my beliefs, but if you can't take a kidding, then there's something wrong either with you or with your beliefs.

I can get back at Porter better than the others. K.P. and I were teammates on the Bullets before he was traded to Detroit for Dave Bing, so I've had a lot of practice at enduring his needle.

He'll be giving me a hard time during a game,

kidding me about my religion and I'll stare down at him (he's a foot shorter than I am) with a scowl and say, like a mother to a little kid, "Now ain't you something? Just look at you." Then we both start laughing and everything's cool.

OUR SENSE
OF VALUES

*A ballplayer should be able to be a
person, like anybody else.* —Dave Cowens, Boston
Celtics

*I hope there's more to my life than
coaching guys in short pants.* —Al McGuire, former
coach, Marquette University

I agree with both of those statements. Two things you're
often reminded about when you're a professional athlete are that you cannot live as other people do and that
the American people have an overwhelming interest,
maybe too much of one, in sports.

Many athletes can understand why Dave Cowens
left the Celtics for two months early in the 1976–77 season. Maybe he shouldn't have done it, but we can understand why. He said he'd "gone stale" even though the
season was still young, so he stayed away for 63 days and
thirty games. You could argue that Cowens supposedly
earns something like a quarter of a million dollars a year
and that for that kind of money a guy ought to be willing to play whether he feels like it or not. You could
argue that a professional is a professional, and you show
up for every practice and every game because of that.
You could argue either one of those points or both of
them, and I'd agree with you, and Dave probably would,
too.

But you have to be what Americans now call a
"superstar" before you can understand why Dave Cowens did what he did and the conditions behind it which
affect every famous athlete and could prompt more of
them to do what Dave did. I think Kareem Abdul-Jabbar can identify with Cowens, too. He told David Du-
Pree of the *Washington Post* that being an NBA star "is
rough on me because, like it or not, I am a personality.

That infringes on my right to be a private person and, for that alone, it's not as desirable as some other situations I can think of."

When Cowens came back the stories said he feels too many people forget that basketball, like any other sport, is only a game. Everybody gets so serious. They give you more praise than you deserve when you win and more criticism than you deserve when you lose. You're worshipped or you're damned. If your team wins, your school or city are giddy with joy. If your team loses, the people go around in gloom and doom. ABC Sports even made a cliché out of it: "The thrill of victory, and the agony of defeat."

Maybe it sounds strange for a guy who owes almost everything to sports to be talking like this. I do owe a great deal to sports and to many decent, intelligent and helpful people who were in sports long before I was and will be long after I'm gone. Basketball has given me my education and financial security for the rest of my life. It has enabled me to plan a life after basketball built around serving God. For all these blessings from sport, I feel grateful.

But I can still appreciate what Dave Cowens and Al McGuire and others have said. There really *is* more to life than basketball or any other sport. There's your family, your religion, your work, there's music and the beauty of nature and the opportunities to help other people and so many things in addition to sports, but they all seem to be forgotten when it's the kickoff of the big game and the kids wonder why Daddy's so grouchy. The fans should leave that deadly seriousness to us pros, whose livelihood depends on our performances. We're serious about it but for good reason. For the fans, it still ought to be fun, and I get the impression it's much too serious with many of them.

As bad as all that seriousness by the fans—and

some reporters, too—are the things we say if our heroes lose. Roger Staubach, last Sunday's hero, is suddenly a bum. George Allen, last week's genius, is this week's jerk. The same writers who were telling us last week our team could go all the way are telling us this week the team is overrated. Elvin Hayes, who scored 40 points last night, is criticized today for not passing.

My point isn't that we shouldn't engage in any of these practices. Sports are great fun—if we let them stay that way—and great stimulants, and everybody in them, including me, is fair game for criticism and second-guessing. My point is that we let our interest in sports engulf us and affect us far more than a game should. And we let them affect others, innocent and decent people, in a damaging way, especially when "he couldn't win the big one."

I've always been amused at the way we throw that one around. "He's a good coach, but he's never won the big one." Or, "He's a good pitcher, but he's never won the big one."

Sparky Anderson had the Cincinnati Reds in the National League playoffs every season for years, "but he never won the big one." Thus, he's not a good manager. Then the Reds beat the Red Sox in the 1975 World Series and—presto!—Sparky Anderson becomes a great manager. I liked what Anderson said before that seventh game. Some of the writers were saying his job might be on the line this time, that he had to "win the big one." It was one of the most exciting World Series every played, and in the midst of all that national excitement and personal pressure on him, Sparky Anderson said, "My best friend is dying of cancer. This game is not the most important thing in the world." A man who keeps his balance like that is a champion whether he wins or loses.

John Madden was an also-ran for years as coach

of the Oakland Raiders. He was a good coach, "but he never won the big one." Then he wins the Super Bowl after the 1976 season and—presto!—he's a great coach. Then there's poor old Bud Grant out there in Minnesota with the Vikings. We still have to say, "He's a good coach, but ... "

It is not only silly and shallow reasoning, it can also be harmful to the individual. You get stuck with that reputation and it influences your progress, how far you can go in your profession, or how much money you make. And there are always cases like Don Newcombe, the great Brooklyn Dodger pitcher of the 1950's. He was a 20-game winner almost every year, but they always said "he can't win the big one." One year he won 27 games but the Dodgers didn't win it all, so it was Newcombe's fault because ... Anytime you win that many games and you're keeping your team in contention all season, you're not only winning *a* big one, you're winning at least *several* big ones.

But they hung that reputation around his neck. Don Newcombe turned to alcohol. Maybe that was one reason and maybe it wasn't, but it sure didn't help him any. He's okay now. Makes you wonder about a few things, doesn't it?

Michigan's football coach, Bo Schembechler, has given a lot of thought to this subject, and for good reason. He had a heart attack the night before his team played in the Rose Bowl. A few years later he underwent open-heart surgery, six and a half hours of it. He views things with a sense of values worth noting. One of his players, Greg Morton, told Leonard Shapiro of the *Washington Post,* "The main thing he taught us is that football can't be your entire life. You dedicate yourself to it but you always leave another door ajar—law school, medical school or whatever. Like Bo says, if you close all the doors you may have to come back one day and you won't have the key to any of them."

He works hard, prepares his team but maintains his balance. His team made another trip to the Rose Bowl—the first season after his open-heart surgery. His preparations that week included taking his seven-year-old son to Disneyland.

The press has a role in this too, for good or bad. Reporters and columnists and announcers can take this obsession with sports and winning even worse, or they can remind us to keep our balance. They can help us with the kinds of words I've just quoted, or they can do us a real disservice by continuing and aggravating not just the clichés in our language but the clichés in our thinking.

I have often wondered, for example, whether any inspiration produced by Vince Lombardi's "Winning isn't everything, it's the only thing" was offset by the harm it might have done. How many high school and college coaches have used that statement to plant an attitude in players' minds that becomes so distorted that the players become obsessed with the need to win and despairing when they lose? How many Little Leaguers have been embarrassed because their team didn't win and maybe it was their fault and so their ten-year-old world is shattered because they're told they have to win-Win-WIN!

Nobody likes to win more than I do. Nobody takes the floor with more determination than I do. Nobody takes better care of his body than I do so we can win. So it's not a case of not liking to win, or not wanting to. It's not even a case of not holding great respect for Vince Lombardi, because I do. On my mantlepiece at our home in Maryland, where I live during the season, is a plaque which I put there because I agree with it and with the man who said it. The plaque reads:

106

> Winning is not a sometime thing. It is an all-time thing. You don't win once in a while, you don't do things right once in a while, you do them right all the time. There is no room for second place. There's only one place, and that's first place. —Vince Lombardi

I agree with every word of that. That's why it's displayed so prominently in my home. But Lombardi was talking to professionals about their performance. He wasn't telling whole cities of hundreds of thousands or millions of people that their world will stop turning if their team loses, and he certainly wasn't telling Little League coaches to bark their heads off at their kids and talk to them the way Lombardi talked to hardened pros.

Maybe it sounds contradictory for me to be saying this, involved in so many big games over the years. I've entered every game, including the so-called "crucial" ones, knowing two things: I'll do everything in my power to destroy my opponent, and the sun will rise tomorrow whether we win or lose. Some writers have misunderstood this attitude, and that inability to understand surfaced again after the Bullets lost to the Houston Rockets in the second round of the NBA playoffs following the 1976–77 season. I want to talk more about that when I cover not just that year's playoffs but other playoffs as well, including our big upset loss to Golden State after the 1974–75 season.

It may sound especially strange for me, of all people, to be talking about getting too hung up on winning and big games when you remember I was one of the central figures in "the greatest game in college basketball history." I remember how important that game was to me at the time, how much pressure I felt to win it, how determined I had been over an entire year to defeat UCLA, how hard all of us worked for weeks and

107

months to prepare to reach that goal. But I also remember being aware that it would not be the end of the world if we lost. I would have been extremely disappointed if it had gone the other way, and so would a lot of other people, but I would not have awakened on Sunday morning with a sense of despair. I have mentioned that after the game, Kareem went to a party with some of the Houston players. Here he was, defeated in this major national event, losing a game for the first time in his college career, and obviously he's not thinking he should go out and hang himself.

Vince Lombardi always managed to survive defeat. Dick Motta, our coach, hates to lose as much as any man I've ever known, but he still endures it. Lombardi didn't like it, Dick doesn't and I don't—but life goes on. And the one nice thing about sports is there's always tomorrow. You strike out this time up, there's always the next time. You miss that shot, but there's always the next one. Have a bad game today, there's another game tomorrow. A bad week, forget it. Concentrate on this week. You can even have an entire bad season, then do what the Dodger fans always used to say—wait 'til next year. Dick Allen, such a great hitter, says he never let an unsuccessful time at bat bother him because he knew it meant he was that much closer to his next hit.

That's what I have to remember. I guess some people think I'm a little too philosophical about defeat, that I get over a loss too easily. But an athlete has to be able to control his emotions. You can't get too high on a win or too low over a loss. If you do, you reduce your effectiveness and your ability to perform for your team. You owe it to the team, your owners, your fans and yourself to maintain your consistency. That's what makes champions, and despair because "we lost the big one" cuts into that consistency and reduces your ability to come back successfully.

108

The press can help us maintain our equilibrium, or it can aggravate the national obsession about winning, about "the big one" and about our preoccupation with sports of any kind. For example, the press will tell us in the papers and on the air that the build-up preceding the Super Bowl is phony and inexcusable and how can anybody fall for all that drumbeating by Pete Rozelle and his National Football League publicity merchants? They tell us it's ridiculous that the TV network can command a quarter of a million dollars for one minute of air time for a commercial, and they tell us it's unbelievable that the NFL expects people to fall for all this.

But they tell us for two weeks. Who's falling for it first? If there isn't any news coming out of the Super Bowl because there's a two-week break to create a publicity buildup, why add to it? And by the time THE GAME finally gets here, we're back to the "winning the big one" cliché. Who will be a genius this time tomorrow because he won the big one? And who will have to drag himself back home stuck with the reputation that he's a failure because he didn't win it?

That's the national mentality which is either created by the press or compounded by it. It's great to get excited about the big game, but let's not make Super Bowl XII as important as World War II.

Al McGuire had some related thoughts on the subject. Even before his Marquette team won the collegiate basketball championship in the 1976–77 season, McGuire said he was going to retire from coaching. He was one of the most successful coaches in the country at the time, still only 47 years old, and he was walking away from it all. He made his announcement in December. When his team won the NCAA title the following March, he didn't

109

change his mind, not even after he established his reputation as a genius by "winning the big one."

He had some thoughts for all of us on that December day when he said he would quit:

> I never look back to the past. I thoroughly believe man is made for more than one career, but it takes a lot of courage to go on to the next one. I'm moving on to another part of my world. I hope there's more to my life than coaching guys in short pants.

The press affects athletes in another, much more direct, way. The writers and announcers can make or break careers by what they say or don't say, and the ones in New York have by far more influence than they should.

Example: In the 1976–77 season, the fans were given the vote to select the two All-Star teams. I've been on the All-Star team every one of my nine years as a pro. I was on this one, too, but not as a starter. The fans picked two other forwards ahead of me: Julius Erving and George McGinnis, both of the Philadelphia 76ers.

I'm sure the fans voted the way they thought was right, and there was no real "get-out-the-vote" campaign to load up the team with Philadelphia players. It was a simple case of the fans voting for the players they thought were having the best years, and that's just my point. They were led to believe that by what they read repeatedly in the papers and heard repeatedly over the air.

It just so happened, however, that neither Julius nor George, two outstanding players whom I respect, was the forward having the best year in the NBA East. I was. Steve Hershey of the *Star* wrote a story about it with a headline which read:

ELVIN HAYES IS AN ALL-STAR—
EVEN IF THE VOTERS DISAGREE

He wrote some nice things about me, right from the start of his story:

> Elvin Hayes has reached that rare level in sports where his outstanding performances are taken for granted. Pete Rose is supposed to get two hits a game, O.J. Simpson is expected to gain 100 yards and Elvin Hayes is counted on for 25 points.

Steve mentioned that, in addition to the scoring which is always expected of me, I was "contributing in many other areas." He quoted Phil Chenier, one of our starting guards, as saying, "This All-Star voting is a joke. The kind of year Elvin is having, he should be one of the starting forwards."

Our other starting guard, Tom Henderson, our playmaker on the point, said some other complimentary things that same season. "I knew Elvin was a good player when we played against him at Atlanta," he said. "We always feared him, but he's doing things now I've never seen before. I never realized how great he is."

Steve quoted my coach, Dick Motta, as saying, "I don't even look at statistics and I know Elvin has been our most consistent player from the first day." Then he said something which holds special meaning to me. He said, "People who said I would have trouble with him didn't know what they were talking about."

If Dick had looked at the statistics, this is what he would have seen in support of his kind words about me. I was:

1. Outscoring both Erving and McGinnis.
2. Averaging more rebounds than any forward in the league.
3. Third in the league in blocked shots, behind only Kareem Abdul-Jabbar and Bill Walton, both of them centers.

111

I finished tenth in the voting. Dave Cowens did better, a lot better. He finished second among the centers—despite his two-month absence.

Now those strange vote totals were not necessarily the *fault* of the press—but the writers and announcers were certainly a factor. They always are. It's true in all sports, especially in the case of television. The announcers have an influence over the careers of the players and coaches to an extent that the announcers themselves may not realize.

If they say a guy has lost a step, that guy is damaged, whether the announcer's personal opinion is right or wrong, because enough people are going to believe it and some will repeat it and pretty soon it's the athlete's reputation, even if the opinion is wrong. Likewise a player will get a compliment from an announcer whose opinion of the ballplayer may be a lot higher than anybody else's in the game. But the same process is set into motion and, again, an athlete's career has been affected, in this case to the good, because his reputation has been affected by the overpowering influence of television announcers whose words are heard by such vast numbers of people.

I'm not saying this is wrong. It's probably unavoidable. But it's dangerous. The great majority of our announcers are experienced, intelligent, well-informed and impartial. But the potential to influence is there, and if any of those ingredients are missing, some good or some harm can result.

The NBA All-Star voting was one example. I know I have benefited over the years because of network television exposure and the kind things the announcers have said about me, and certainly that huge TV audience for the Houston-UCLA game helped launch me on my pro career. But take the case of Julius Erving. Julius is an outstanding pro basketball player, always has been. But he was also a pro basketball player in New York.

Until the two leagues merged and Doctor J demanded a renegotiated contract and wound up in Philadelphia, he was playing in front of the New York writers and announcers—that includes the Associated Press, United Press International, *Time, Newsweek, Sports Illustrated,* CBS, NBC, ABC, *The New York Times.* Everything comes out of New York.

In the case of television announcers whose networks cover NBA games, there is as much opportunity to ignore a player as there is to showcase him. I'm one of the fortunate few. I've always received attention from the announcers and their cameramen, but others aren't so lucky. You're hearing about Rick Barry and Doctor J and Pete Maravich and Nate Archibald and Kareem Abdul-Jabbar and even Elvin Hayes, but some of the men playing the best ball in the league go unnoticed. They're the young players.

While the announcers were still raving about John Havlicek when he was 37 years old and nowhere near the player he had been, guys like Billy Knight, John Lucas, Calvin Murphy, Jim Chones and Campy Russell weren't getting nearly the kind of coverage they should have. It's as if the superstars are the only players in the league. If you're going to cover the league, cover the whole league, not just five or six players. I don't buy that, or the heavy exposure for New York athletes and New York teams. How many times on Monday night football do you hear Howard Cosell talk about Frank Gifford when he was a New York Giant or about Y.A. Tittle or Joe DiMaggio or Micky Mantle or Yogi Berra or the New York Knicks of the Willis Reed era? Everything is New York or the established few names.

George Foster probably agrees with me, or would have reason to. He carried the Cincinnati Reds in

1976 with a tremendous year, so who gets voted the National League's Most Valuable Player? Joe Morgan, for the second time. Joe's a friend of mine from the days when we both played in Houston. He's a fine man and a great player, but in my opinion one of the reasons he won the award was because he had won it before. He had his name and his previous years going for him. That's fine. Nothing wrong there. But in this case a player is overshadowed because of the media's attention to someone else.

That's wrong. If a player wins an award or is voted to an All-Star or All-Pro team or is considered one of the great current players, he ought to be getting that recognition on the basis of what he is doing. He should deserve to be there. The news media shouldn't just give one guy a free ride and ignore someone else who may be better but happens to be playing in Indiana instead of New York.

Officials are another group who can affect your performance and your career, maybe more in basketball than in other sports. In pro football six officials supervise the game. In major league baseball there are four umpires, six in the World Series. In basketball the number is two. The whole game—played at a faster pace than any other team sport except hockey—is officiated by two men. If either of them is incompetent or has it in for a particular player or team, he can have a direct effect on your performance and even on the outcome of the game itself. He may not mean to, he may not even realize it, but it can happen—and does—and sometimes they certainly seem to realize it.

Some officials seem to work differently if they know the game is on TV. They make more calls, they slow down the game and in general they seem to be much more prominent. They're performing. Nobody is coming to see them or turning on their TV set to watch them, but they're performing anyhow. The good officials like Earl Strom and Richie Powers won't do this—they're good and consistent every game—but a guy like Mendy Rudolph will have a little showmanship in him. Mendy was a capable official, but he was also a bit of a performer, more than Earl and Richie are.

A couple of officials even seem to have some problems with their attitudes toward blacks. When Dick Motta became our coach he asked us early in that season, "What have you guys done to these officials?" One explanation that has been suggested is that we had been coached for the three previous years by a black man. It's a terrible thing to think in this day and age, but some of the players and coaches have wondered about it, and Kareem Abdul-Jabbar has even mentioned it in public. He came right out one year and said he thought certain officials were prejudiced and that they would never give him a break on a foul call.

I know there are some players in the league who never seem to get a break from the officials. Norm Van Lier is one of them. So is Eric Money. And Kevin Porter. Those poor guys just seem to get picked on all the time by the officials.

By the same token, certain other players in the league seem to get favored treatment from the officials. Whether they mean to do it or not, the fact is that some guys just get away with murder in this league. Dave Cowens is one of them. Bill Walton is another. And Maurice Lucas and Bob Lanier. All those guys can beat on you and pound you all night and they get away with it. They have the officials intimidated.

Other players seem to have the officials psyched out another way, making the refs think they're always being fouled. Nate Archibald and Rick Barry are two examples. Nate is a fine young player who can do a lot, but he almost doesn't have to bother with field goals.

He'll score 39 points and 20 of them will be on free-throws. And Barry. It's almost useless to try to defend against him. You're going to be called for a foul anytime the two of you barely come into contact. That must be how he became such a good free-throw shooter. The refs sure give him enough practice.

I guess every player feels he gets picked on more than he should be, and I'm no exception. A few years ago, one of the reasons may have been the troubles I was having and the reputation the San Diego writers were giving me. I think some of the refs—not all of them, but some—viewed me with an attitude which said, "I'm not going to give him anything."

I think that reason probably has disappeared gradually over the years, but I also feel that some officials still don't give me any the better of it, just as other players feel the same way about their own cases. In my case, I think the reason now is they see I won't bow down to them and I won't play according to their likes and dislikes. I play my own game night after night. Even when I get into foul trouble I don't alter my play. I must have more playing time with five fouls than anybody else in pro basketball, but I never back off at that point. I still drive to the basket with the ball, I still fight for the rebounds, I still go up to block my man's shots and I play just as aggressively as anyone else on the floor. And I don't often foul out.

Besides, if I hold back, that's stealing from the public. The fans pay their money to watch the pros and I'm not going to let the officials or anyone else deprive them of the fun they came to see.

Some officials just seem to get too impressed with their own power. They can curse at you and give you a lot of verbal abuse, but you can't even ask them about a call in a civil manner without risking a technical foul. Instead we're told we can't say this and we can't say that to the officials.

The inconsistencies in officiating complicate your life, too. One night you'll go out and everything is beautiful. The officials are letting you play. The next night you can't touch anything. That just shouldn't be. Even allowing for the human factor, there should be more consistency in the calls than there is. You shouldn't have to adjust your game from night to night depending on who's officiating and what kind of mood they're in.

That's what happens, though. You have to ask, "Who's working tonight?" Even if it's the same two who worked last night, there's no guarantee they'll call it the same way tonight.

In one game last season, an official at half-court called a foul on me while I was under the basket. There was no way he could have seen that action unless he was Superman and could see right through the other players. I asked him, "Why don't you cross that line and get on top of the game?" He called a technical on me.

One of the frequent complaints by a player is not that he didn't foul his man but that the official was out of position and couldn't possibly judge or see accurately. Fans don't realize this, but many times that's what the player is griping about, not the foul itself but the poor position of the referee to see it.

They called three fouls on me in the first quarter of that game, plus that technical. I still scored 40 points, because I wouldn't alter my style of play just because of the officials.

Another time last year we were playing Cleveland in an important game and the refs called four fouls on me in the first quarter. Dick Motta took me out to save me for later and then sent me back in.

As I came back onto the floor at half-court from

the scorer's table, I said to one of the officials, "Can I play now?" Tweet! Technical foul! Number Eleven! The officiating was so bad in that game the Cleveland fans were booing the refs in the last quarter, and their team was winning.

A technical foul usually says to me that the officials have lost control of the action at least temporarily. It shows you've embarrassed one of them, usually by exposing an incompetent call, and his retaliation is to call a technical against you. I know it's true in my case. I don't scream at them. I don't curse them because I don't curse period. So the technical can't be for unsportsmanlike conduct. It's because I've embarrassed him or insulted him by pointing out his mistake.

Baseball players can question the umpire all game long. Football players can, too. In basketball, it's a technical foul.

When I was playing in last year's All-Star game the inconsistencies in officiating flared up again. Because I had finished tenth in the voting for forwards while having what the writers and everyone else were calling the greatest year of my career, I wanted to play in the worst way. I wanted to give the fans a real show. I was up as you can be for a game and I showed it with my shooting. I made my first six shots—zip, zip, zip—I have 12 points and it's still early. Doctor J and some of the other guys were beginning to tell me I was headed for the Most Valuable Player Award. Then the officials started calling them tight on me. Before you know it, I'm in early foul trouble and I watch most of the rest of the game on the bench, even though on three of the fouls called against me, I never touched my man.

At the same time this was happening, I'm getting knocked around all over the place because I'm the guy doing the scoring. I asked one of the officials why he wasn't calling those fouls and his answer was, "It's just an All-Star game. Let them play. It's all right." So there we were again, playing in front of a national television audience in a game where the fans want to see the stars perform and never mind all the whistles and the interruptions for foul calls, yet we were caught in the inconsistencies. That's what really bothers you about the officiating. Call them one way or the other, but call them all the same way.

This isn't just a complaint from one player. It's the feeling of many players and coaches in the NBA. Like Golden State's coach, Al Attles. The Warriors beat Buffalo but Attles was upset. His team did not shoot a free-throw in the second half. He said, "I cannot believe that in pro basketball, with all that pushing and shoving, a team cannot have a man at the free-throw line at all in the second half."

And Houston's coach, Tom Nissalke, voted Coach of the Year in 1976–77, said after his Rockets were eliminated by the 76ers in the playoffs that year, that the officiating "just made me sick."

While I'm talking about fouls, let me mention one particular call which ought to be thrown out, and I want to make my pitch right here to do that. That's the charging foul where the defensive player plants his feet just in the nick of time and lets his man charge into him for a foul against the offense. That practice, which is encouraged by coaches all the way from kids' ball to the NBA, should be dropped.

The Atlantic Coast Conference stresses it. It's a poor excuse for basketball. It encourages too much faking, doesn't require any ability and, worst of all, creates too much of an opportunity for serious injury. Many players, coaches and general managers have called for that foul to be dropped from the rule book, and I've been told that Red Auerbach, who built and coached those champions with the Boston Celtics, is one of those who have tried the hardest.

In the pros, with guys 7 feet tall and 225 pounds charging into each other, one of them flying at full speed while the other is stationed firmly in his way, somebody's career is going to be ruined. You take a charge against a guy like Wes Unseld or Darryl Dawkins or Bob Lanier and you get a round of applause from the fans and a compliment from your coach, but you might be lying out there on the floor with your career at an end.

People ask me about changes in the rules to improve the game. I think the people responsible for making the rules have done a good job. Pro basketball is a great show now for the same reasons pro football is. There's a lot of scoring, it's a fast game, it's exciting and it's a physical-contact sport, regardless of what people might tell you. The 24-second clock and the rule against zone defenses, which isn't always enforced, have made it possible for us to put on a fun game for the fans.

The only improvements would be to throw out that foul encouraging charging and to require the officials to be more consistent in their calls.

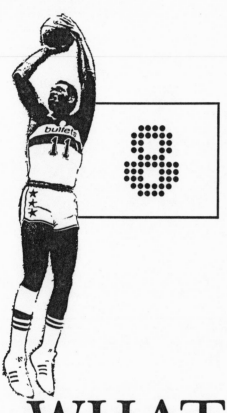

WHAT "NBA" REALLY STANDS FOR

Being a professional athlete is the greatest thing that could have happened to me. It's made so many good things possible for my family and me, both now and in the future. I think most of the other players in the NBA would also admit that they're plenty lucky—at least I hope they would—living a glamorous life and getting these fancy salaries.

But the physical routine sometimes makes you forget your good fortune. The only thing you remember is that you're tired. The traveling in pro basketball is a killer. I never have understood why we don't do what baseball does, play two or three games in a city on the same trip. That would cut down considerably on the hotel bills and the cost of all that jet travel and seems to make good business sense. It would also spare us players a lot of days when we're almost dead on our feet.

Instead, we play one-night stands all year long. The only time we play more than one game in a row in the same city is when we're home. Otherwise it's play one game, fly to another city, play another game, fly to another city. No wonder some guys in the league say "NBA" stands for "Nothing But Airports."

Steve Hershey of the *Star* gave a good description of a typical NBA road trip last season. We were in San Antonio after a game with the Spurs. It was Christmas Eve morning. We got our wake-up call at 6:45 and met at the airport at seven. We waited one hour for takeoff. Then we flew to New Orleans. There we had a layover which lasted two hours. On the flight home from there we lost another hour when we crossed the line from the Central Time Zone to the Eastern. We arrived at Baltimore-Washington International Airport at 3 P.M., seven hours after meeting at the San Antonio Airport. I got home at about four o'clock.

The next afternoon, Christmas, we had to leave our families and play a game that night against Cleve-

122

land, which we won, 117–99. The next morning we met at B-WI airport at 7:30 to fly back to New Orleans. The weatherman was calling for snow, so we had to get up early, between 5:30 and six, after not being able to get to bed until after midnight because of our game. The flight was delayed because of ice on the runway. The delay lasted three hours. Then we flew to Dallas on a special flight, changed planes after another delay of seventy minutes and arrived in New Orleans in midafternoon for a game that night. It added up to three games in four days in three cities.

That was an exhausting experience but it's really not all that unusual. Another time that season we beat Indianapolis out there, got back to our hotel about 12:30 or one o'clock in the morning, were called out of bed at 5:45, arrived back at Baltimore-Washington International at nine in the morning, played a game at home that night at 7:30 against Cleveland and took off the next day for another road trip lasting seven days.

It's all part of the job and you just have to put up with it or find another line of work. Nobody says you have to like it and nobody really enjoys it, especially all that A.T. (Airport Time), but you have to get used to it.

In a way, I prefer to play on the road because I'm spared all the interruptions and distractions you get at home, with personal appearances and people calling you. On the road you can keep concentrating on your job and prepare yourself for the game coming up. I read the Bible and watch TV or go to some friend's house—and I make sure I take an afternoon nap so I'm rested and strong, trying to make up for the fatigue of all those airplanes and the A.T.

But I'm not just a road player. I can play at home, too. In fact, my greatest scoring game as a pro came at home. I was a rookie with San Diego and had been playing pro ball only one month when I scored 54

123

points one night, against Detroit, mostly against Otto Moore (the guy who's only an inch under 7 feet whom the Rockets later obtained because they were so anxious to get a big man at center).

I kept taking Otto outside that night, beating him with my quickness and hitting with a lot of jump shots facing the basket, layups and everything else. But I couldn't have done it without my point guard, Art Williams. Art was penetrating the Piston defense and I was getting open and together we were unstoppable.

Art was one of the best point men I have ever played with. The best was also in that game. He was George Reynolds, the guard who did so much for me when I was a senior in college and he was running our offense. My point total at Houston went from 881 points as a junior to 1,214 as a senior. My scoring average jumped from 28 points a game to 37 points, and the reason was George Reynolds.

George was on the bench—the other bench—most of that night. He had been drafted by a team that didn't need another first-string guard because they already had Dave Bing and Jimmy Walker. Kevin Porter and Tom Henderson have also been great point guards for me to work with, but George Reynolds was unquestionably the best. And yet his "career" in the NBA lasted only half a season.

Although I'm known mostly for my scoring, I take pride in the other phases of my game, too. I try as hard as I can to play a good defensive game, to block shots and get some steals and grab rebounds, to do all those things whether I'm scoring or not. Usually when I don't score my average, the press will say, "Elvin Hayes scored only 17 points" or, "Elvin Hayes was held to 15 points." That always sounds as if I had a bad night, that I didn't contribute much, but often I've had a good night in those other parts of the game besides scoring.

One night I grabbed 35 rebounds, and on many other nights I'll grab 20 or more. It's a source of pride to me that only eleven other players in the history of the NBA ever grabbed 10,000 rebounds before I reached that mark a few months ahead of my teammate, Wes Unseld. I think it's a convincing answer to those people who criticize me by saying I'm not aggressive enough or I'm too hung up on religion to be a part of the violent phase of pro basketball or all I can do is score. Over 10,000 rebounds in only nine seasons, an average of more than a thousand a season. You don't pile up stats like that unless you're in the middle of the action slugging it out with everybody else every night.

Some nights the ball seems to come off the rim right to you. You feel extra strong and everything is cool. Other nights you block out your man underneath the basket, get good position—and the ball goes the other way all night.

Rebounding is a stimulating part of the game. I find it enables me to be aggressive, to turn violent in a way I can feel good about it. I let off some steam by going up in the air and attacking the ball and yelling like somebody in a cowboys-and-Indians movie. It feels good, as if you're climbing to the top of the world, conquering everyone below you while they reach up with their hands and try to catch up with you and can't. It gives you a sense of exhilaration, knowing there's a group of men below that basket reaching and pushing and shoving and jumping for something, and you're beating everybody.

You get the same kind of stimulation from making a slam-dunk, only that can be a two-edged sword because if you miss the shot, the feeling of embarrassment is just as strong as the stimulation is when you're successful. As exciting as rebounding is in letting out all your frustrations and feeling that you're conquering the world, the slam-dunk turns on those feelings even more.

It looks easy, but it's not. I've always said that two of the most difficult shots in basketball can be the slam-dunk and the layup. Any shot from only two or three feet can be hard if you don't have the correct angle at the basket, and sometimes that's what happens when an opportunity for a dunk or layup opens up. The ten-footers are easy. You're close enough and usually you have the angle and you just pop it. They're easy shots. You should be able to make them all night.

But with layups and dunks, you're driving your way to an opportunity in close, and when it opens up you're not always at a good angle but you're so close you feel you have to put it up anyway. Sometimes you should go back out with it, but that often is a hard decision to come to when you have the ball 24 inches from the hoop. So you feel compelled to go up with it and when you miss everybody says you "blew the shot." The announcers are great ones for saying it that way. "So-and-so blew the shot." There's a difference between missing a shot on a good try and "blowing it." Sometimes you do blow one, but it's not true every time you hear it described that way. The same way with a team's lead. If you're winning by 20 in the second half and you lose the game, then I think it can be said that you blew a lead. But if you're ahead by 3 with two minutes to play and you lose, that's not necessarily blowing the lead. It means you just lost, that's all. I draw a difference between losing a game and blowing one, just as I do between missing a shot and blowing one.

After all, to blow one means that you had everything all wrapped up and there was just no way you could miss or lose, but you managed to find a way anyhow. That's blowing it. And when you say a player or a team "blew it," you're using an insulting term and making an accusation. It's a term that people, especially announcers, often use inaccurately and unfairly.

And if you miss the slam-dunk, you'll certainly be accused of blowing it. People ask me why even go for the dunk, why not stick to a straight layup? The answer is that a slam-dunk just fires you up so much and can have the same effect on your whole team, like a home run in baseball. That's why you take the risk and go for it. Look at Bill Walton and the effect his two dunks in a row had when Portland got its first win against the Philadelphia 76ers in the 1977 NBA finals. Those dunks told everyone that Philadelphia was a gone gang for that game.

If you're getting pushed and shoved and knocked around out there, you can let out all your anger by challenging your opponent, taking him to the basket, then making the slam-dunk over him. That's when it really feels good and you know you got your revenge the most satisfying way possible, by showing your man you can beat him in a dramatic contest under the basket.

But when you miss it, man, that's embarrassing. If you have a bad angle and you slam it up there, if you happen to be off just enough in your judgment— POW!—that ball comes firing back out of there and you want to crawl under the floor and hide until everybody has gone home. As stimulating as that shot can be to you and your team, a miss can be just as powerful in its effect on you. It can take you right out of things. You're still in the game, but you're not contributing anything because you're still steaming about that missed dunk three minutes ago. That feeling can then start to feed on itself and you're messed up for the rest of the game because of a missed dunk shot, and maybe your team is, too.

I missed a slam-dunk in a game once against

Seattle, and K.C. Jones immediately came up off that bench and called time out. He came over to me and told me, "Hey, forget that dunk. Go back out there and get it right back, but don't let the miss bother you. Just stay cool and keep playing basketball." That was the only reason for the time out, to make sure one of his players who had just missed a dunk would not let it lead to a bad game and maybe a loss for the team.

I went back out onto the court. Just a minute or so later, I stole the ball, wheeled around and headed for that basket. I was going up when I made the decision to dunk it, and I was determined there was just no way I was going to miss this one. I slammed it down through the net and ran back downcourt feeling a whole lot better about things.

In fact, I felt so much better I made four shots in a row. We won the game. That slam-dunk turned it around for us. The dunk can do that. It can help you win, just as a miss can contribute to your defeat. It's hard to believe that one shot can have that much effect on the result of a game, but in the case of the slam-dunk it's true.

In addition to those two dunks against Seattle— one good and one a miss—I guess the other dunk I remember best is the one I never got to take. We were playing the Celtics, and Kevin Porter, our point guard at the time, called a play designed to get the ball to me at the hoop for a dunk. The play starts with me picking my man, then rolling off the pick to the basket for the pass from Kevin.

The guard was John Havlicek, and he never missed a trick out there. After I picked my man, I started to roll past him. Havlicek was just a few feet in front of me guarding Porter when, out of the corner of his eye, he saw me starting my roll behind him and off my man.

Just as I figured the play was working, I had beaten my man and was headed home free and easy with 2 points coming up, I suddenly felt this tugging. Havlicek had reacted quickly. He whipped around and grabbed my pants at the waist. There we were—I was tugging one way trying to get to the spot where the pass was going to be, and Havlicek was pulling in the opposite direction and really hanging on. He wouldn't let go, so my pants started to come down. Kevin saw what was happening and knew the play had been stopped, in Havlicek's own way, so he called time out. Good thing he did. If that struggle had gone on much longer, somebody might have been arrested.

The most colossal dunk I ever saw, maybe the most exciting one anybody has ever made in a scary way, came one night when Philadelphia was playing Seattle. Lucius Jackson stole the ball and headed straight for the basket, all alone except for Bob Rule, who was trying to catch up. Lucius went up for the dunk and slammed it home while Rule, still trying to catch him, ran under the basket and off the court because of his momentum.

Just as both players found themselves out of bounds and behind the backboard at the end of the play—BOOM!—the whole glass backboard exploded. The glass shattered into a million pieces all over the floor. It was a miracle that, of the ten players in the game, eight were still too far away to be hurt and the other two were on the other side of the blast, just far enough in the opposite direction to miss getting cut to ribbons.

Rule was the luckiest guy of them all because he was trailing Jackson and had gone under the backboard just a split-second before the glass exploded. I was in the stands, and it still is the most stunning thing I ever saw happen in a basketball game.

Another thing almost as surprising—maybe "impressive" is a better word because it involved ability, but it was plenty surprising, too—came in a playoff game between the Lakers and the Celtics. I was still playing with the Rockets in San Diego, so I drove up to Los Angeles to see the game.

Elgin Baylor drove toward the basket on one play, went up for the shot, showed Bill Russell the ball in one hand, shifted the ball to the other hand and made the layup against the greatest defensive center in the history of the sport.

A few minutes later, the same thing started to happen. Elgin, who is one of the all-time greats just as much as Russell, took him on again. Here are these two true champions again going at each other in a test of athletic greatness. Baylor makes his move to the basket, goes up with the ball, shows it to Russell in one hand, switches it to the other hand and prepares to complete the layup when—BAM!—Russell blocks the shot just as clean as you please.

But that wasn't all. Bill picked his own blocked shot out of the air, went the full court with it by himself and scored at the other end.

Russell was always so good and so aggressive. That's why he had always been my favorite player while I was in high school and college. I always heard more about him anyhow, because he was from so close to Rayville, but it was his aggressive style of play that made me like him so much, plus, of course, all that natural ability and leadership.

Bill Russell was so fast, not just big, that I saw him once do something that I don't think anyone else could ever do. Jerry West, a great player himself and a guy who never wasted any time in getting a shot off, was near half-court when he decided to bomb one from out there. He was just great enough to do it and did, all the time.

This time he released his shot when, all of a sudden, here comes Russell, racing all the way from underneath the basket up to West at half-court in time to block the shot. The ball went out of bounds. I know it's hard to believe, but I saw it. Nobody else in basketball that I know of could do that. They say I'm quick, and at 6-9½ I'm tall enough to block a lot of shots and do. I'm among the leaders in the NBA every year in that category, but I cannot imagine myself on my greatest day ever coming close to being able to do what I saw Bill Russell do on that play.

In fact, it was in the same game when he made that great play against Baylor. That block against West, when Russell was all the way down at the basket as Jerry started to get open to take his shot, has to be one of the greatest demonstrations of athletic skill anybody in that arena has ever seen.

That's the kind of thing they would have put up against me as a comparison if I had accepted that scholarship offer from the University of San Francisco and tried to follow in the footsteps of the great Bill Russell. No, thank you. After watching those superman plays in that game, I was glad I picked the University of Houston. I didn't need my college career to consist of four years of being compared to that kind of greatness.

9

I BELIEVE

The life of the professional athlete is dotted with personal appearances, some free, some for pay. The players on the Bullets, like those on many other professional teams, are asked to make at least two free personal appearances a year for a worthy community cause. For Elvin Hayes, two is never enough. He feels a strong urge to do more, and has always done so in San Diego, Houston, Baltimore and Washington. But more is still not enough. Already the Bullet making the most free appearances, Hayes told the Bullets' director of press relations, Marc Splaver, several years ago that he wanted to do still more for charity groups, especially for those organizations working with kids.

Splaver, a respected figure himself who has been voted the outstanding public relations director in the NBA by his professional colleagues on the other teams, is emphatic about the contributions Elvin Hayes continues to make to his community.

"Two Bullets," Splaver says, "have won the Professional Basketball Writers' Association Citizenship Award for community service in the three years that this national award has been given, but the Bullet who, to my knowledge, has done far more work in the community than any other is Elvin Hayes. I have never seen a superstar so willing to devote his time, free of charge, to worthy causes."

Marc Splaver should know. He handles the schedule.

Elvin Hayes, traveling from October into May and out so many nights for games even when the team is at home, has sacrificed his evenings to appear free at banquets for the Multiple Sclerosis Society, the Catholic Youth Organization, No Greater Love in honor of Vietnam veterans missing or killed in action and other organizations, churches and schools. The list is so long that Marc Splaver will tell you, "There have been so many over the years that I simply cannot remember them all."

134

*Elvin Hayes has done more. He has served as
"I.Q. Chairman" (I Quit Smoking) for the American Cancer
Society. He has devoted a great deal of time and effort
to the D.C. Society for Crippled Children. The Bullets'
correspondence file shows a letter reporting that, in a year
when other Easter Seal agencies suffered "substantial
losses" in contributions, the Crippled Children's Society
topped the previous year by $8,000. The letter, to Hayes
from John D. Husband for the Society, says, "The
reason we did not meet a similar fate, I believe, was your
contribution of time and the cooperation you and Marc
Splaver gave us. It was fantastic and we are delighted and
grateful. People alluded to your television spots in notes
accompanying their contributions and, as far as I know, that
hasn't happened before."*

*The TV messages for Crippled Children are one
in a long list of public service announcements for television
which The Big E has recorded without charge. He has
taken the time to go before the cameras to make appeals in
behalf of the United Way, the Special Olympics for
retarded children, Muscular Dystrophy and all those others
too numerous for Marc Splaver, Elvin Hayes or
anyone else to remember.*

*The Hayes message is no commercial sales pitch to
hustle tickets to Bullets' games, nor is it a hellfire-and-
brimstone alarm to get straight with God tonight because the
world ends at nine o'clock tomorrow morning. Instead,
the Hayes message, like the man, is a quiet word on physical
health, spiritual health, helping others and finding God. The
specific message depends on the nature of his audience.
It is a measure of both Elvin Hayes and his popularity
among the people of Washington and Baltimore that the
flood of requests for him keeps on coming.*

What I say to an audience depends on who they are. If
I'm talking to a high school or college audience, I tell

them that they can conquer life's hills if they have a foundation to their lives. I tell them how lucky all of us are to be living in America, the greatest country on earth. I say that because, regardless of what country we happen to live in, God put us on this planet for a reason, to serve Him and give glory to Him and to love our neighbors and help them in every way we can. This is the foundation in life which I feel we all need. I tell my young audiences that, with this foundation, everything is possible, because God will be with us and will bless our efforts in accordance with His will. And I mention that, without this foundation of love for God and obedience to His will, our lives will never fulfill the potential which God gives to each of us.

Another point I emphasize to young audiences because I feel so strongly about it is the obligation which the young people of every American generation have to repay this nation for the blessings and freedom we enjoy here. I remind them that we came into this world in a nation of wealth and opportunity and liberty, and if we are to deserve these blessings and keep them for ourselves and our children, we should be prepared to serve our nation, our community, our church or whatever. By making contributions to our community and by trying to set an example as good citizens, we can make some small repayment for the freedom and opportunity which our parents and their parents have passed on to us.

When I'm talking to the American Cancer Society, I have a different message—don't smoke. The only time in my life I ever smoked was when I was nine years old. I made my own "tobacco" from a fig tree in our yard, then stuck it in a corncob pipe and went fishing, just fishing and puffing. That stuff tasted so awful I've never again had any desire to smoke. The same thing has helped to keep me from drinking. I've tasted alcohol on two occasions. Once was that time I drank a little champagne at my sister's wedding reception, then went home and ate some watermelon and almost killed myself. The only other time was at a party when I was in the tenth grade. Somebody had mixed some Schoolboy Scotch, which we called "Thunderbird." They were passing it around in an alley near my house. I grabbed the bottle because I was anxious to see how it tasted. I got my answer before even one swallow. That stuff tasted so bad that my taste buds must have jumped straight up and intercepted it because I turned my head and spat it out as fast as I could, without a drop going down my throat. I haven't tasted a drop of alcohol since.

In the case of liquor, it's easy for me to stay away from it for another reason. I still remember all that drunkenness and violence and all those alcoholics from my childhood, so I'm not about to fall into that trap, not even this many years later. Those poor people lived only for Saturday night so they could get blind drunk. That was their ultimate goal.

In the case of cigarettes, I tell audiences of the American Cancer Society that I have strong feelings against smoking because of what I saw it do to my father. It gave him a lot of sickness and it took him from us at an early age. Even though I was only in the ninth grade when he died, I still remember very vividly all the times he tried to quit, but he kept going back to it. He puffed and puffed and blew himself away.

I don't believe in being obnoxious about that sort of thing. If somebody wants to smoke or drink or whatever, I believe that's their business unless they're breaking the law or bothering me in some way. Otherwise, I feel it's their life to live the way they want. But on smoking I do tell my audiences that I know you probably can't find 100 percent factual evidence that smoking causes cancer, but the evidence is so overwhelming that any jury would conclude there is enough proof.

I also tell my school audiences that an athlete really has to be foolish to fool with cigarettes. They're no good for you as a ballplayer. They cheat you. They can shorten your wind and they can impair your nerves, especially if you smoke heavily. You're endangering your ability to perform. That's how smoking cheats you. You're hurting yourself, your team and your family. So my advice to my audiences on this subject is simple: Don't smoke, especially if you're an athlete or want to become one.

When I make appearances at hospitals for the Crippled Children's Society, I don't offer a message—I receive one. I see those kids sick and incapacitated, some of them crippled so much it takes a superhuman effort just to lift one little finger. All their hard work and dedication just to be able to move that one finger, and I can lift all of mine at once.

I can't really give them anything. I get something from them instead. Sure, I can give them my time and put on a happy face and help them forget their problems for a while. But I'm really the one being helped. Those crippled little kids are telling me, without knowing they're doing it, how lucky I am that God has blessed me with a body which is whole and healthy and I realize again how fortunate I am to be able to run up and down a basketball court time after time, night after night, to be able to jump up in the air for a shot or a rebound—and some of those kids have trouble just sitting up in bed. That's the message and the new inner strength I get from my visits to those kids in their hospitals and institutions, and that's why I'm so glad that I am able to help crippled children in any way possible.

In all my appearances I talk at least briefly about my belief in God. I honestly think there is a religious renewal starting in the United States which is helping us to rededicate America to God. The news reported not long ago that the Gallup Poll people have found that America is on the edge of a real boom for religion, an unusually strong movement by many Americans back to God and their religion. I think President Ford helped to start this move by the good example he set both in the White House during the week and in church on Sunday. I think President Carter is adding to this awareness of God and prayer. Those two Presidents didn't necessarily start this turning back to God, but I'm sure they are helping it. I think all of us as individuals and as one united country are going to be better off because of this rededication.

The feeling I have that America is returning to God and to the beliefs of our fathers isn't just a hunch of mine, or a public-opinion poll by George Gallup. There was another story in the paper recently saying that attendance in most churches in every section of the nation is up, and many people I know who are active in their churches tell me the same thing. And I get it all the time in my personal appearances, especially with the young people. So many of them are turning to God, and many others are searching for Him and a way to Him. I can tell you two true stories which illustrate why I feel this way.

One night a couple of years ago I was speaking to sixty or seventy students at Fairleigh-Dickinson College in New Jersey. It was storming outside, but inside, in the cafeteria, we weren't talking about the weather. We were talking about Christ and heaven and hell and love of God. A young man, not a Christian, wasn't saying much but he seemed to be paying extra close attention to what I was saying. All of a sudden he got up. I could see tears on his face. He didn't say a word. Instead, he ran right out of the building and into the dark night and that heavy storm. His friends told me he was a nice guy who was always laughing and teasing and clowning around, but this time he didn't seem to be fooling. They said he didn't worship God, that the only thing he worshiped was his stereo equipment in his room. They said he was absolutely crazy about that stereo and all the gear he had to go with it.

Well, he not only surprised everyone in the room by getting up and leaving with tears in his eyes and walking out into that storm, he really messed up one guy because the one who walked out had his buddy's car keys in his pocket.

That young man who left our group in tears wandered around outside all night. I don't know how his friend ever got home, but I guess he did. But when this stereo fanatic came back the next morning, he said his life had changed overnight. He said that what I had been talking about—needing God and loving Him and dedicating ourselves to Him so our lives can have a foundation and a purpose—really took effect on him. His friends said they were sure of that, because he would never before emphasize something like that over his stereo equipment. But here he was, finding God and forgetting something worldly which had seemed so valuable to him before.

In the second story, I was in Jacksonville, Florida. I had talked to a few young men the night before. Early the next morning there was a knock on my door. It was one of the guys I had spoken to the night before. He said he just wanted me to know that he had prayed the week before for God to send him someone with the answers about God and faith and love. He said I had brought those answers.

I'm nobody with any magical message. It isn't any power from me that gets through to people like those two young men. It's God's power. I've been able to see through these happenings and so many other testimonials and witnesses that people are looking for God and finding their way back to Him. I also know that these happenings prove once again that there is a God. If trees and flowers and the change of seasons and the beauty of the mountains and the magic of the stars aren't enough to make a believer out of you, all you have to do is witness the response of people like these two young men when they hear the message of God.

After my basketball career is over, I hope to spend a lot more of my time and energy doing as much as I can to continue helping to spread the word of God. Maybe it will be as a minister or as an evangelist or in some other capacity. I don't know which yet, because I don't know yet what God's will is on this subject. Whatever way He chooses, I'll be helping to spread His word in the Houston area and wherever my travels in His name might take me.

As a matter of fact, I did some traveling in His name this past summer. I went to Arizona for about ten days to meet with some others to see how much we could do to increase the number of professional basketball players in the Fellowship of Christian Athletes. Many of the ballplayers in pro football and major league baseball belong, but only a few guys in the NBA are members. Those of us who are want to correct that.

It's a cause consistent with my Christian beliefs. The Fellowship describes itself in its monthly magazine, _The Christian Athlete,_ as "a movement to confront athletes and coaches, and through them the youth of the nation, with the challenge and adventure of accepting Jesus Christ as Savior and Lord, participating in His Church and serving Him through our vocations."

That sounds serious and lofty, and I'm sure some people suspect that only religious freaks could join an organization which describes itself that way. But

141

some pretty manly and physically tough customers belong to the Fellowship of Christian Athletes and devote their time to those goals—people like Tom Landry and Roger Staubach of the Dallas Cowboys, Bert Jones of the Baltimore Colts and Terry Bradshaw of the Pittsburgh Steelers in football and Brooks Robinson, Jim Kaat and even the Commissioner, Bowie Kuhn, in baseball, and guys like Bobby Jones of the Denver Nuggets in pro basketball. And the Fellowship isn't limited to players and coaches. The general manager of the Philadelphia 76ers, Pat Williams, is one of the most active members of the FCA.

The Fellowship of Christian Athletes is the kind of organization which I can enthusiastically identify with. You hear about it when writers and broadcasters are telling you about a famous athlete who happens to belong to the FCA and does a lot of good work in the community. But the FCA really works first of all with the junior high and senior high school athletes, helping to bring them together so they have an opportunity to talk about their concerns, their fears and anything else. They call these groups "huddles," and there are two thousand of them at junior and senior high schools around the United States. The same kind of groups are also established at colleges all over the country. At the college level the FCA calls these groups "fellowships." There are fellowships on 400 college campuses.

These groups are not just therapy sessions for athletes to talk their way through their troubles. They also feature Bible study, prayer, discussion and service. They are established to encourage athletes to influence society as witnesses before other young people. From these huddles and fellowships, this emphasis by the FCA on spiritual help and service produces visible as well as moral results in the form of rest homes for senior citizens, Big Brothers programs for fatherless boys, the

Special Olympics for retarded children and other programs aimed at spiritual advancement and service to your community.

It's just like my firm belief that there is a God because of what I know and see and read. The Fellowship of Christian Athletes is another piece of proof in my mind. In addition to these 2,000 high school groups and 400 more in college, there are 325 adult chapters of FCA. It all adds up to more than 10,000 high school, college and professional athletes participating together in Christian beliefs and Christian works because of their belief in God. Just like the boy in New Jersey and the one in Jacksonville, when I see evidence like this, I know there is a God and that He has a role for me in this life. That's why I went to Arizona to meet for ten days with some of my fellow NBA players to see what we can do to increase the number of pro basketball players who are active members of the Fellowship of Christian Athletes.

The one personal appearance I'll never forget came on February 15, 1976. That was when I delivered the invocation for a Presidential Prayer Brunch for Professional Athletes at the White House. It was a Sunday, and President and Mrs. Ford were both with us in the East Room, plus the Marine Band. Erna came with me, and we both got to meet the Fords and talk to them. It was a real honor to receive the invitation, especially to be asked to deliver the invocation.

Jim Kaat, the baseball pitcher, was there. He stood up and told us his definition of a "religious fanatic." He said, "That's someone who knows Jesus better than you do." There were more than a hundred professional athletes there who knew Jesus. They heard speakers like Kaat, Kyle Rote, Jr., Madeline Manning Jackson, the runner, Norm Evans of the Miami Dolphins, Rik Massengale from the pro golf tour, Dennis

Ralston from tennis, Calvin Jones of the Denver Broncos and Janet Lynn Salomon, the figure skater.

They heard Calvin Jones tell the story about W.C. Fields, the comedian, reading the Bible on his deathbed. When someone asked him why he was all of a sudden reading the Bible, he said, "Looking for loopholes, looking for loopholes."

But we weren't there for laughs. We were there to give serious expression to our commitment to Christ, not just the speakers. Out in the audience were the rest of the hundred athletes—Bert Jones, Jim Hart and Jim Plunkett from the National Football League, Andy Messersmith, Bill Madlock and Kaat from major league baseball, Joe Frazier from boxing, Billy Cunningham and I from basketball, and two of the biggest coaching rivals you can imagine, Tom Landry and George Allen, who slug it out every year in the NFL's Eastern Division.

I was lucky enough to be invited back, for Erna and me to have dinner with Queen Elizabeth and the President on the Fourth of July to celebrate America's Bicentennial anniversary. We went, and it was a great and proud evening for us and for America, but the prayer brunch with President and Mrs. Ford had just as much meaning because we were giving honor and glory to God.

Madeline Manning Jackson was one of the speakers. She said, "My thing is running for Jesus." She does it well, because she won a gold medal at the Olympics in the 800-meter event. Norm Evans, the lineman for the Dolphins, said something significant: "When football players say yes to God, we discover blessings that are far more important and exciting than being world champions or All-Pro."

Jim Kaat stood up and talked about his "commitment to God to make Him the center of my life." He told us, "That gave me peace, purpose and direction."

All told, there were between 200 and 300 people there, athletes and their wives and other guests. Out of the then 26 teams in the National Football League, twenty were represented on that beautiful day at the White House. Out of the then 24 major league baseball teams, seventeen were represented. I'm not the only professional athlete with serious religious beliefs.

The President told us, "I have always had envy for you who have made it in athletics." He said he still reads the sports page first every morning, before turning to the national and international news on the first page. Earl Warren, the Chief Justice who died a few years ago, was another high government official who once said the same thing.

President Ford also told us, "What you said and how you said it meant a great deal to Betty and me, and all of us. No more outstanding representation of athletic prowess ever has been seen in this house before. You are special because of your love of God, your faith in Him."

When I delivered the invocation, I prayed:

Oh, Heavenly Father, we thank You for the opportunity to honor Your name.

It is only fitting that this take place in this, our Bicentennial year, as we are gathered here at the White House in our nation's capital to reaffirm our beliefs in the principles on which this nation was founded, those principles which were based on a deep faith and trust in God, our creator, and in his son, Jesus Christ.

Bless our nation and our nation's leaders, for Your word says blessed is the nation whose God is the Lord.

We thank You for the presence of all the athletes here today, whom You have so richly blessed with diverse talents. Let this be a time of rededication for all of us.

And, Father, I pray that not only our bodies be nourished, but that our souls and spirits be enriched by the words that go forth here today.

In Jesus' name, Amen.

Erna and I wrote the prayer together.

SECOND
SEASONS

The NBA playoffs, called pro basketball's "second season," have not always been happy times for Elvin Hayes. As his coach, Dick Motta, puts it, "It seems that whenever the Bullets lose in the playoffs, Elvin gets blamed." He could have added: "by the reporters."

When the Bullets lost to the Houston Rockets in the 1977 playoffs, the reaction was predictable. The old myths were dusted off from last year and put back into the typewriter and on the airwaves: "Elvin Hayes always chokes up on the playoffs. He's the reason the Bullets lost. He just never does well in playoff games." That was the charge against him, but the way it was said told you something else.

One writer wrote, "What Elvin Hayes needs to do is give himself a cold slap in the face." The same reporter also wrote, "When things are going well, Hayes goes well. When they are going bad, Hayes goes bad."

Another writer, this one a veteran old enough to write with maturity, wrote, "Losers are expected to destroy lockers, to run over unleashed dogs and to firebomb the neighborhood. It is not desired, but it is understood."

Not by Elvin Hayes it isn't. And not be Dick Motta, either. That was the reason for this column. Hayes and Motta had both said the Bullets lost to a better team and that's all. Hayes added, "I don't think we disappointed anyone. We just didn't win."

The same columnist actually said, "This is the basketball big league, Elvin, not the sandlots." He really wrote that.

And just as predictably as everything else, that writer dusted off the Vince Lombardi quote, you know the one we mean: "Winning isn't everything, it's the only thing."

And he quoted George Allen, the Redskins' coach, "Losing is like dying." Research might show that the same columnist climbed all over Allen for saying that

*originally, but now he was holding it up before the citizens of
Metropolitan Washington as a model attitude. The
Elvin Hayes response to his friends: "I haven't seen anybody
yet fall over dead just from losing a ballgame."*

*A third writer joined the newest game in town
by saying in his column, "The difference between Hayes in
the regular season and Hayes in the playoffs is the
difference between E and e."*

*But is it? Entering 1977's "second season," here is
the Hayes playoff record, stacked up against Kareem
Abdul-Jabbar, the NBA's player of the year four seasons out
of the last five.*

HAYES		ABDUL-JABBAR
42	Games	57
24.7	Scoring Average	29.7
49%	Shooting Percentage	51%
66%	Free-Throw Percentage	70%
12	Rebound Average	17

*Hayes' scoring average is just 5 points below Abdul-
Jabbar's and only 1 point below Rick Barry's. His average is
5 points better than Dave Cowens has been able to do
in playoff games. Beginning with the 1973–74 season, two
other categories—steals and blocked shots—were added
to NBA statistics. Here is the comparison for those categories
in playoffs.*

HAYES		ABDUL-JABBAR
36	Steals	20
82	Blocked Shots	39

*Amid all the furor by the writers, who seemed more
upset than the readers, almost to the point of paranoia, it
remained for someone 3,000 miles away from
Washington to provide the real reason for the Bullets' loss to*

149

*Houston in the '77 playoffs. Jerry West, an NBA
standout for years and now the coach of the Los Angeles
Lakers, watched as his team lost four games in a row in
those same playoffs to the Portland Trail Blazers. He was
talking about the great Abdul-Jabbar. "Kareem is
great," West said, "but he can't do it alone." Elvin Hayes
agrees with Jerry West.*

It's always easy to blame one guy. That's the coward's
way out. Twelve guys win and twelve guys lose. It was
the fault of twelve guys that we were on vacation after
the Houston series instead of playing the Philadelphia
76ers. It was the fault of every player and it was Dick
Motta's fault and it was Bernie Bickerstaff's fault. And
when we win the NBA championship, it won't only be to
Elvin Hayes' credit. It will be to the team's credit.

We never had this problem of pointing the finger when I was in the playoffs with San Diego or the
Bullets in our earlier years. Nobody expected us to go
all the way. With the Rockets it was a miracle just to be in
the playoffs. We never had any reason to feel disgraced
after I came to the Bullets, either. We were drawing the
New York Knicks at their peak and the Boston Celtics,
who still had enough greatness in them to win, so nobody gave us much of a chance anyhow. That's why the
writers weren't screaming for the Bullets to get rid of
me or demanding that the players "destroy lockers, run
over unleashed dogs and firebomb the neighborhood."

The closest we've come yet to that championship
ring was when we reached the NBA finals against
Golden State in 1975. It was just our luck that it turned
out to be one of the biggest upsets in NBA playoff history. Everybody was saying we'd roll on to the title and
make quick work of the Warriors. And we felt the same
way. We were not overconfident, but we were good and

150

we had every reason to believe that we would win it all against Golden State.

That was an extremely exciting and gratifying year. We stormed our way through the regular season with a record of 60 wins and only 22 defeats. We commanded respect throughout the NBA. Then we drew Buffalo in the first round of the playoffs. The Braves had a tremendous scoring machine that year, led by Bob McAdoo, the NBA's leading scorer that season, and we were going to have to be at our best to beat them.

That series reached a crucial point after McAdoo scored 50 points one night in Buffalo and the Braves evened the series at two games each. We were coming back home to the Capital Centre with an absolutely "must" game facing us. If we lose this one, we're down three to two and returning to Buffalo and it's just about all over. But I scored 46 points that day—not bad for a guy who never plays well in the playoffs—with a lot of help from my teammates, especially Kevin Porter, who was doing an incredible job of knowing when I was open and then getting the ball to me. That's what it takes, teamwork, and we had it when we needed it. We went on to whip the Braves in the series, then beat the Celtics to reach the finals against Golden State. Bob Cousy was broadcasting those games against the Celtics. This man, with all those great playoff performances of his own while Boston was dominating professional basketball, said he had never seen the Celtics so outplayed in a playoff game. That's how good we were, and how together we were.

Nick Weatherspoon was sensational in that series. He kept coming off the bench with a hot hand at the other forward spot and really helping to keep Boston at a distance. Up there he was driving the fans nuts. They couldn't understand how a kid substitute in only his second year in the NBA could be doing this to their Celtics. A friend of mine was in Boston a month after that series and he said the writers were still taking potshots at this guy they had never heard of who had played such a key role in eliminating their team.

We didn't even let Boston take us to seven games. We beat them in six. There we were, having played two of the top teams in the league in the first two rounds of the playoffs, also the two fastest, and we beat them both. We were ready for Golden State and that championship.

But we lost something more important than one game in our last win over Boston. We lost Jimmy Jones. Jimmy was our third guard. He was a good playmaker who was able to keep our offense running, just the way Kevin could. He was tall—6 feet, 4 inches—and an excellent shooter who had just come to us from the ABA. People felt the Bullets had scored a real steal when Jimmy came to us, and I agreed. I knew all about him because he played at Grambling, fifty miles from Rayville, and I was familiar with what he had done there and had followed his progress in the ABA. I knew how great he was and how much he could help us. He did, too.

Other teams would try to get Kevin mad—K.P. has been known to have a temper at times—so they could get him out of the game. He not only quarterbacked our offense, he ignited it. He would beat the other team downcourt and penetrate and either take the shot or dish it off to an open teammate. Other teams figured without him our offense would sputter, and normally that reasoning would work—except when you have a Jimmy Jones. He kept filling in for Kevin all year and we kept winning. Spoon was doing the same thing at forward. We were winning because we were balanced, with a bench that was delivering, and we were together, all twelve of us. Nothing could stop us now. But—

In the closing minutes of our final win over Boston, John Havlicek was driving for a layup. Jimmy moved up to block the shot and John came down on top of him. Jones was hurt, and right away you had the feeling it was bad. Jimmy was helped off the floor. We were anxious, especially the five of us in the game, because we didn't have any information on the injury, whether it was serious or something minor but painful. We almost blew the win we were so worried about Jimmy.

Our worst fears were justified. Jimmy had seriously injured his knee. He was out for the Golden State series and maybe even finished for good. It was a terrible blow to the team and an awful piece of luck for any guy, especially a good guy and a good player like Jimmy Jones.

This information, naturally, meant something to Golden State. It meant one of our strongest performers off the bench wouldn't be bothering them. So the Warriors came out trying to get Kevin mad so they could either destroy his effectiveness or get him out of the game. Kevin was able to keep his cool most of the time, but even an aggressive and well-conditioned athlete like K.P. has to come out of there for a breather once in a while, and when he did, Jimmy Jones wasn't there.

To make our problems worse, Weatherspoon was as cold against Golden State as he had been hot against Boston. Spoon was still in there trying, maybe too hard, and he really wasn't helping us much either, although it wasn't his fault and there was nothing he could do about it but just keep on shooting. But the shots never did drop for Spoon in that series. So there we were with Jimmy Jones and Nick Weatherspoon both unable to help us, playing against a coach who believed in using everybody and wearing down the opposition. That was Al Attles' strategy and it worked. Our starting

153

five beat their starting five, but their bench wore us out. Clifford Ray and Derrek Dickey and others just ran us into the ground while we were playing basically six men.

Even so, we were confident before the first game and before every game after that, even the last one, when we were down, three games to none and facing overwhelming odds. We still felt we could do it. We still knew we were good and we thought we could win, even without the strong bench which had taken us such a long way. We were apprehensive about Jimmy's absence, but we still really believed in ourselves, and in each other.

We tried to put fear into them right away in that first game, to psych them out and remind them that here they were playing the Bullets, who had won 60 of 82 games and were the heavy favorites to win the championship. We wanted to go right at them, to attack them early and scare them. It was working, too. In that first game, we ran up a 14-point lead right away, playing on our home court and with the crowd with us. Things looked ripe for us to go one up in the series right off the bat and make them unsure of themselves. That way we could dictate to them for the rest of the series and get those championship rings.

But even with our big lead and our crowd screaming for us, those guys on Golden State just wouldn't quit. They kept coming back and kept closing the gap, closing the gap, and finally they won the game. From then on, the whole momentum shifted to the Warriors. We'd start off in good shape, but that bench that Al Attles kept throwing at us would wear us down eventually, and there was Jimmy Jones with his knee in a cast and Kevin Porter still in the game with his tongue hanging out. Attles knew the situation and took full advantage of it in every one of those four games. That's how

154

we lost to Golden State in one of the biggest playoff upsets of all time in the NBA.

But even losing a championship we were favored to win didn't produce all the fuss and insults that hit the papers and the sportscasts after our loss to Houston in the '77 playoffs. You would have thought from the reaction that we had been favored to win that series instead of the one against Golden State two years earlier.

Maybe the reporters—some of them, not all—were building up to it after we followed our upset loss to Golden State by losing to Cleveland in the first round of the playoffs the next year. After that year, in which we won only 48 regular-season games compared to those 60 wins of the year before, K.C. Jones was fired as our coach. I didn't agree with that decision, and I wasn't afraid to say so. The papers reported it, and that was fine with me. I thought K.C. was and is a fine man and an outstanding professional basketball coach. It wasn't his fault we hadn't done better, but in pro sports if you don't do as well as some people think you should, the coach gets fired or the star gets traded, or both.

So Kase was gone, and it was a real shame. He had so much class, and he had helped me so much, just as Gene Shue had before Kase. And I'll always remember Kase talking to us after our final loss to Golden State. He told us it wasn't anybody's fault in particular, that we just got beaten, that we missed Jimmy Jones, and Golden State came out on top, but we should look forward to next year. All of us felt the same way, and we knew that, even though we had not won the championship, we had a champion for a coach. He wasn't telling us what the writers told us two years later, that we should go out and commit suicide because we lost to Houston. It's easy to show class in victory, but it takes a real man to show class in defeat. That's just the way Kase was.

So after dropping to those 48 wins and that first-round loss to Cleveland the following season, Kase was fired and Dick Motta was brought in from Chicago to get us going again. He did, even though we were off to a slow start. We didn't win any more games than we had the year before under Kase, but considering the slow start while we were learning a brand-new system of offense, I'd say we did all right and no one had anything to be ashamed of.

We played the best basketball of any team in the NBA over January and February, then hit a five-game losing streak in late March but pulled out of it in time to get into the playoffs. People forget, but there was a time during Motta's first year here when the writers were expressing some fear that we wouldn't even make it to the playoffs. But we didn't panic, something Coach Motta keeps emphasizing to us—to keep our composure—and we got straightened out in time.

We would have preferred to win the division championship over Houston, but we didn't and we couldn't spend the playoffs moaning about that. We had to go out and play. We had developed our offense under Coach Motta and had improved ourselves with three excellent young additions Bob Ferry brought to our team, Mitch Kupchak, Larry Wright and Tom Henderson. Mitch and Larry were rookies, Mitch from North Carolina and Larry from down home at Grambling. Tom came to us in midseason from Atlanta in a trade for Leonard Robinson.

So there we were, a new head coach, a new offense, and three new key players, ready to take on Cleveland in the playoffs, the same team which had eliminated us in the first round the year before and cost K.C. Jones his job.

This time the pleasure was ours. We knocked them out in three games, with Tom Henderson playing a sensational final game after having a bad night against them in the second game in Cleveland. We came back to Capital Centre on a Sunday and Tom just tore them open. He scored 31 points, I had 23 and Cleveland was gone.

Then came Houston. The Rockets had the home-court advantage and they came out in that first game aiming to make full use of it, believe me. They ran up a 15-point lead early in the first period. The only point we had was a free-throw by me. We were on the ropes and it was still the first quarter.

But we got things together in the second period and played them right off the floor, the same way they had done to us in the first period. It was two different basketball games, both in the same half. We were trying to get within a respectable difference by the half, so we went to work on that huge Houston lead, and instead of getting to within 10 points or so by the half, we found ourselves within 4. Then Phil Chenier scored with just a few seconds left in the half to cut it to 2. Larry Wright intercepted their inbound pass and dumped it off to Wes Unseld, who made the layup as the buzzer was sounding. We had a tie, an incredible comeback, all of it accomplished in one quarter instead of needing the whole second half to overcome such a tremendous Houston lead. It was a great comeback and a great boost for our morale and our chances.

Then, in the second game—we're still in Houston—we lost a game we should have won, this one in overtime. Still, we had started the series knowing we were going to have to split to maintain our chances coming back to Washington, and that's what we had done. So we had accomplished our objective, and everything still looked cool.

But then we fell behind in the series, even while playing at home, and never did catch up. We lost the final game on a Sunday afternoon, at home, and it was all over in six games. Well, in a way it was all over. In another way, it was just starting.

The papers had been saying, and some of the announcers, too, that the reason the Bullets weren't doing better in our series against the Rockets was that I wasn't scoring. Well, I scored 50 points in our last two games against Houston, and we lost them both. The complaint had been made over the year, over many years, in fact, that the Bullets are too inconsistent, that they can never hold on to a lead, that they always get a big lead but then blow it. But Coach Motta, who has been a head coach in this league for ten years, will tell you that a big halftime lead is one of the worst things that can happen to you in the NBA because the team will usually let up in the second half and start taking poor shots instead of staying in their offense and working just as systematically as when they were running up their big lead in the first half.

The Bullets aren't the only team in pro basketball like that. They're all like that. It's a characteristic of pro basketball. Once that same season, Cleveland was playing the 76ers on national television and had a 22-point lead in the last quarter—and still lost it. In the NBA, it happens.

On the same day we were losing to Houston, Denver, with one of the best regular-season records in the NBA, was being eliminated by the Portland Trail Blazers, 108–92. There wasn't much doubt in that game. The Blazers led by 25 at one point. The Nuggets cut it to 11 with a minute and 46 seconds left, but Portland was still not seriously threatened. Looking back now, I wonder what the reaction was in Denver that week. David Thompson scored only 17 points for Denver in that game. I wonder if the papers were saying the loss was

158

his fault. That he didn't contribute his share. That he's not a valuable member of his team.

The Lakers were next on Portland's list, and they didn't even win one game. That was when Jerry West said no one man, not even Kareem Abdul-Jabbar, can do it alone. In one game, Kareem got to take only twelve shots. I wonder if they were saying in Los Angeles that it was all Kareem's fault. I doubt it, because in some of those games he was scoring 40 points, but they still lost.

There were several reasons for our final loss to Houston. Two of them were Rudy Tomjanovich and Mike Newlin. They scored 47 points between them— and I don't guard either one of them. In the fourth quarter, the Rockets were taking 22-footers and hitting everything they put up. Even shooting from that distance, they shot 75 percent from the floor in that last period. Now that's nobody's fault at all. That just means they have a 6-10 center under the basket named Moses Malone and those guards and forwards bombing from downtown know when they put it up that if it doesn't go in Moses is going to use his 6-10 height to get the rebound and put it in anyhow. That's why Houston is one of the best-shooting teams in the NBA. What can a forward guarding his man down low do when a guard is standing at half-court and dropping them in as if he has radar?

But the reaction set in, just the way I knew it would, with some of the writers making their annual comments. Some writers aren't above getting personal, either. The same *Star* columnist who had zinged me before with so much pleasure could not resist the temptation to go to the well again. He outdid himself this time. All the writers in Washington are aware of my religious attitudes and that I take my beliefs seriously

159

and leave everyone else to his own. So this guy calls me Goliath in his column and says, "Goliath couldn't win the big one either."

That's not only a personal cheap shot, it's the same old emphasis on judging an athlete (or a coach or a team) a success only if he wins "the big one." Here the Bullets are in the playoffs for the last nine years in a row, the only team in the NBA with that honor, and we're getting rapped every year because we don't go all the way. That writer has never won a Pulitzer Prize either, but I bet he considers himself a good writer without it.

I know the Washington fans themselves don't always agree with some of the things they read in the paper. I know from friends of mine who have lived here for years that they are still thankful just to be in the playoffs. In the case of basketball, they're thankful just to be in the NBA. They've had an NBA team only the last four years. In the case of baseball, they don't have a team at all. I'm sure it's not their fault, but you'd think they'd be grateful for what they still have, and the fans are. But some of the writers seem to overlook the fact that they could be covering nothing but soccer, and how many guys on one paper can cover the same team?

It pops up with the Redskins, too. They were a nothing team for 25 years, a quarter of a century of losers. Not even Vince Lombardi could get them into the playoffs, and he was the only superman who could even bring them a winning record. But they were so bad from 1946 until 1971—25 years—that they tell me people used to drive around with bumper stickers that said, "Bring Pro Football Back to Washington." That's how bad they were. Then, with George Allen as their coach and Bill Kilmer as their quarterback, they were in the playoffs five of the six Allen-Kilmer years, and once they made it all the way to the Super Bowl.

Would you believe they at times get a terrible press? They criticize Allen for all sorts of things, then make fun of him because he likes ice cream and drinks milk and says, "Goldang it." So what? And they criticize Kilmer for one reason: Because he's not Sonny Jurgensen. So what? Who is? They talk about his wobbly passes. They don't look nice. But he's a winner and a leader who gets his team into the playoffs, the place the Redskins never got to, not even the year they had Vince Lombardi as their coach and Sonny Jurgensen as their quarterback.

The *Washington Post* conducted a survey of the area's sports fans a few months ago. Allen and Kilmer may get a bad press, but the fans like them. Eighty-five percent of them said Allen was doing a good or excellent job, and Kilmer was rated the second most popular player in Redskin history, behind only Jurgensen.

One year Kilmer actually came out of a hospital bed in real pain with a bad stomach, quarterbacked the Redskins in a crucial game, got them into the playoffs with that win, then climbed back into his hospital bed, still in pain. Still they rap him when everything doesn't go the way some of the writers think it should. It's really strange the way some writers react when the team they're covering loses. You'd think they were the ones missing out on that extra playoff money, not us. Nobody tries to lose deliberately, for the fun of losing. I hate to lose as much as Lombardi or Allen or anybody else on this earth—even as much as some of the writers. So why tear me up, or Bill Kilmer or George Allen?

I don't feel that writers and broadcasters have to be cheerleaders. In fact, I don't think they should be. But I *do* think they should be fair and impartial and not rap one player just because they're friends with another—or because we lose in the playoffs.

But that's what happened after the '77 playoffs. The fans came to my defense, though, the way they always have. The *Star* ran letters to the editor on its sports pages for three straight Sundays which defended me and criticized some of the writers. They recited my statistics and mentioned that I do a lot more besides scoring. They talked about my work on defense and rebounds and in passing and setting picks. One fan said in his letter to the editor that I was "a dedicated team player."

One fan wrote, "It is wrong to blame the failures on Hayes. He scores, defends, rebounds, blocks shots and steals. What more could you ask for?"

But I felt I had put up with enough criticism and abuse every time the Bullets don't win the NBA championship. Bill Kilmer had the same reaction at the end of the previous football season, when the Redskins lost in the first round of the NFL playoffs. He said he was tired of putting up with some of the writers and the booing he gets at RFK Stadium. He said he wanted out, he wanted to be traded. That's what I said, too.

I really love the Bullets, and I'll do anything to win an NBA championship for Abe Pollin and his wife. Those things I said about them earlier in this book, I really meant all of that. But a guy can take only so much. Even guys like Kilmer and me who can take an awful lot of abuse have our limit. I felt I had finally reached mine. And if some of that trash the writers were saying about me was what the Bullets believed, too, then they'd be better off getting someone else for the job.

I requested, and got, a special meeting with Abe Pollin. As you might expect, it was a successful meeting. Abe said he didn't want to trade me, that he wanted me here with the Bullets. He said he didn't agree with those

162

things that a couple of writers had written about me. He said he felt I was a valuable member of the team.

A week after our meeting the reporters finally found out about it, and they wrote that I had changed m mind, that I had "reconsidered." That made it sound as if I were some guy who couldn't make up his mind from one week to the next whether I wanted to be traded or not. It also adds fuel to the charge that I'm a moody person, temperamental, hard to get along with. Well, I can put up with that, so I didn't mind the way they reported it and expressed the reasons for my change of mind. But the fact is that the real reason I felt so much better about staying—I had always *wanted* to— was that now I felt more *able* to.

It's not much fun to read those things about yourself in the paper that some of the writers have been saying about me, so it came as some relief when Coach Motta and Bob Ferry, our General Manager, came back from a business trip out West and came to my defense when they heard about all that had been going on.

Bob said he thought I was coming off my best year. He said I was a hard worker and that I get the Bullets into the playoffs every year.

Coach Motta said more, and some of the things had special meaning to me. "I'll be truthful," he said. "A lot of my friends warned me. But they were wrong. I thought he had a great year, a tremendous year." He told another reporter, "I thought Elvin and I had a good relationship last year and I hope it continues. I know we never could have won 48 games without him."

Coach Motta said he agreed with the NBA coach of the year, Tom Nissalke of Houston, that I get the Bullets to the playoffs every year. Coach Motta said, "We can't afford to give up somebody like that."

Then, when the player draft came, the same *Star* columnist wrote not one but three stories saying I would

163

be traded to Buffalo for Adrian Dantley. Steve Hershey, who covers us for the *Star,* never wrote it, but this guy did. After the draft, Bob Ferry said, "Every move we have made has been centered around Elvin being here next year. There's no question that, surrounded by the right people, he can be a valuable member of a championship team. But he's only 6-9. He can't do it alone."

The record was straightened out on something else that same week. The NBA All-Star team was picked by the writers and broadcasters for the whole league—not just East and West. The results differed from the vote of the fans. The men voted as the two best forwards in pro basketball: Elvin Hayes and David Thompson. Second team: Julius Erving and George McGinnis.

So everything got squared away and we started a new season, which is the way sports should be because that's the way life is. If you get knocked down, if you suffer a defeat, whether it's large or small, you have to look ahead, you have to dust yourself off and come right back, or you'll never be a champion, only an also-ran, just another name down in the middle of the standings.

That's why I couldn't understand that other writer's violent reaction when I said I didn't think we disappointed anybody, we just didn't win. That didn't mean I enjoyed it. I'm not out there getting beaten on and pushed around and stuck with elbows just to lose, but when I do lose I have to have enough composure and maturity to do the job next time out.

K.C. Jones sure didn't like it when we lost that championship to Golden State. With a coach it's especially trying because it's his responsibility to see to it that the team wins. And Kase grew up in the Celtic tradition of winning. He had thirteen notches on his belt. He knew how to act when you win, but he also knew how to act when you lose. He kept our chins up and in that dressing room after our final loss to the Warriors, Kase had us already anxious to start the next season

That's the way it should be, in sports and in life. Jimmy Carter would never have won the highest office in this country if he hadn't been able to accept defeat earlier in his career. Life is full of success stories like that, of people who were defeated, but they didn't panic the way some of our writers did after the '77 playoffs. Instead, they kept their cool and went right to work on coming back.

That's what the Bullets and I are doing right now. I'm going to continue playing just as hard as I know how—and that's plenty hard—and just as much as I know how—and that's a lot, too. In the 1977 season I led the NBA in minutes played, the fourth time I've done it in my nine years in pro basketball. Many a night I'll play the full 48 minutes. And when we go into overtime, it's not unusual for me to play the full 53 minutes. And in nine years of professional basketball, with 82 games a year plus the playoffs, I've missed a total of four games. Nine regular seasons, our playoff games and nine All-Star games all add up to 802 games, and I've missed four. Four out of 802. I don't think any other player in professional basketball can equal that number of games, or the combined record of that many games while playing that many minutes in those games.

I'm confident that the Bullets will come back and do even better than make it to the second round of the playoffs. We've done better than that in the past, and we can do better than that in the future. Coach Motta has had time to install his offense and make sure we all know it thoroughly and can execute it the right way.

165

He's worked three young and outstanding players into our attack and added Bob Dandridge, so I don't see any reason for despair.

But it doesn't depend on just us, the coaches and the players. It depends on God, too. That will sound corny to some people, and it's the kind of statement a writer can have some fun with at my expense, but I believe it, so I don't mind saying it. I honestly believe that nothing happens in this world without God's consent. From the mightiest events in the history of the universe, like the moment of creation itself, to the tiniest things like whether I make my next foul shot, all things depend on God's will. That I believe.

It is this belief that has enabled me to experience whatever success I have achieved. And it is this belief that has enabled me to endure the rough spots in life's hilly road, and when you're a prominent public figure like a well-known athlete, there are many rough spots, like my problems in San Diego and my troubles in Washington after the 1977 season.

I don't go around thinking I am the greatest basketball player ever born. I believe I'm good, but I also believe that I can't take all the credit for that— because God made me good. I don't believe that He sat on a throne up in Heaven and snapped His fingers and ordered a miracle by declaring that Elvin Hayes down on earth would grow up to be a good basketball player. I do believe, though, that He saw to it that various events would take place and would put me on a road which would take me to that role in life. I don't doubt that at all.

I believe God saw to it that I would be born of good and decent parents who would pass on to me the attitudes and beliefs that God wishes for all people. I believe He saw to it that I would go to the University of Houston and be helped so much by Coach Guy Lewis and his assistant, Harvey Pate, and that even before that time, the Reverend John Calvin would enter my life and guide me to basketball in God's name.

And I believe that, if it is God's will, the Bullets will win an NBA championship with me providing some of the help. But if it isn't God's will, nothing else can make it happen, not even all the sportswriters in the world.

I don't know what awaits me after basketball, because God has not chosen to make that clear to me yet. One thing He has made clear, though, is that He wants me to continue to work in His service in some capacity spreading the message of God and Christ in my hometown of Houston. I know that by the time my playing days are over, and I hope that isn't for several more years, He will make it clear to me what my capacity of service will be.

For the present, though, I feel I am doing God's will by being out there on the basketball court, by playing my absolute hardest every game. I couldn't have the records I do in playing time and only four games missed in nine years if I didn't believe it was God's will for me to be out there and if I didn't have His strength to sustain me. I know it is also His will for me to continue to serve the people of the Washington community in every other way possible, to make all the public appearances I can, to work with kids and high school and college students, and the elderly and the sick and the poor, to help Him spread His message of faith and hope and charity for all people.

I'm very happy in Washington, even with the occasional bumps in the road. I've always tried hard to do my best for the Washington team and the Washington people. That's why it hurts when you get kicked in the teeth for supposedly not caring or not trying, just because the team has lost. I do care and I do try, because

167

of Abe Pollin and the rest of the Bullets' organization and because of the good fans of the Washington-Baltimore area.

I'm glad Abe and I were able to work out our problem after the '77 playoffs. I promise him and I promise our fans that I'll never stop playing and hustling and praying for an NBA championship for the Bullets.

If it is God's will, it will happen—and He'll give each of us the ability to make it happen. That's why we shouldn't panic and overreact at temporary setbacks, even when we get eliminated and the season is all over. We can start working on the next season already. When this book comes out, we'll be in a new season and aiming again for the playoffs, for the year's "second season."

When I started this book, one of my goals was to help people see that professional athletes are not just overpaid robots but real human beings with real successes and real failures and real emotions and real burdens, just like everyone else. I wrote this book because I wanted to speak out on certain issues, to set the record straight on a few things and to tell people of my love for God and my belief in Him.

I hope I have achieved these goals in these pages. And I hope the Bullets' fans are convinced, if they weren't before, that I'll always work with all the energy and ability God gave me to win a championship for them. I hope our fans believe that of me, despite what they might read or hear.

I don't kid myself. I'll always be a controversial player, partly because of some of my past troubles and partly because reporters come to me and I tell them what I think. Writing a book can help to set the record straight, I hope, but it won't change my nature as a controversial figure. I can accept that. It's part of the price you pay.

168

All things—success, controversy and the rest—are easier for me to accept now because of the faith I have found in God. I face the rest of my basketball career, and the rest of my life, with complete confidence because I know I'm doing God's will. That's the only reason I'm on this earth.